PITTVILLE
LEARNING CENTRE CHELT

SURVIVING
YOUR
DISSERTATION

SURVIVING YOUR DISSERTATION

A Comprehensive Guide to Content and Process

Kjell Erik Rudestam
Rae R. Newton

FCH LEARNING CENTRE
UNIVERSITY OF GLOUCESTERSHIRE
Swindon Road
Cheltenham GL50 4AZ
Tel: 01242 714600

SAGE Publications
International Educational and Professional Publisher
Newbury Park   London   New Delhi

For information address:

 SAGE Publications, Inc.
2455 Teller Road
Newbury Park, California 91320
E-mail: order@sagepub.com

SAGE Publications Ltd.
6 Bonhill Street
London EC2A 4PU
United Kingdom

SAGE Publications India Pvt. Ltd.
M-32 Market
Greater Kailash I
New Delhi 110 048 India

Printed in the United States of America

Library of Congress Cataloging-in-Publication Data

Rudestam, Kjell Erik.
    Surviving your dissertation: a comprehensive guide to content and process / Kjell Erik Rudestam, Rae R. Newton.
        p.   cm.
    Includes bibliographical references and index.
    ISBN 0-8039-4562-0 (cl).—ISBN 0-8039-4563-9 (pb)
        1. Dissertations, Academic—United States. 2. Report writing.
    3. Research—United States. I. Newton, Rae R. II. Title.
    LB2369.R83 1992
    808'.02—dc20   92-14932

        97 98 99 00 01 14 13 12 11

Sage Production Editor: Diane S. Foster

Contents

Preface

The completion of a master's thesis or doctoral dissertation is usually the most difficult academic requirement a student will face during his or her term of graduate education. The process requires discipline, independent initiative, creative thinking, working with others, and the surmounting of self-doubt. It is no wonder that many A.B.D.s never become Ph.D.s. Completion of the dissertation is simply too overwhelming for many.

Surviving Your Dissertation: A Comprehensive Guide to Content and Process represents our combined efforts to facilitate the dissertation process among our students. Our experience comes from working not only with our own students, and discovering our own mistakes, but also from listening to others. The positive, self-affirming experiences and the "horror stories" have both served to develop our thinking. Unfortunately, the social organization of the dissertation experience is not one that is well understood by most students or their faculty mentors. The expectations are often vague, the norms unclear, and the social networks among student, chair, and committee members incomplete. While it is expected that graduate students in the social sciences will have mastered the intricacies of research design and methodology, it is not as likely that they will be systematically exposed to issues of appropriate style and content of the dissertation. As such, we have witnessed the many frustrations that students may experience along the dissertation trail: how to select a suitable topic, how to conduct an appropriate review of the literature, how to build an argument, how to manage data overload, how to work with faculty committees, how to organize time and space, and how to deal with emotional blocks to completing the project.

In response to these challenges, we have developed some useful strategies for managing the process toward a favorable outcome. Success comes from an understanding of what a dissertation contains, and an understanding of one's own strengths and weaknesses. We characterize the first as an understanding of *content,* and the second as an understanding of *process.* Mastery of the dissertation depends on the ability to negotiate both process and content successfully. This book is organized around these themes. In Part I we discuss how to select a topic and possible methods by which a topic might be approached. In Part II we focus on content. We describe the dissertation chapters, what they might reasonably be expected to include and not include, and how to present that material appropriately. We provide detailed directions for describing the research plan and presenting data and results. In Part III we address issues of process, including common barriers to progress. Separate chapters discuss task and emotional blocks, use of a personal computer and computer software to complete the dissertation, the presentation of numbers, and ethical issues.

Surviving Your Dissertation is not a substitute for courses and texts in research methods or statistics, but a comprehensive "how to" compendium for completing a master's thesis or doctoral dissertation. It should be appropriate for any graduate student about to face this major academic challenge, and may prove useful for many faculty about to direct such endeavors. Throughout this book we have tried to be broad in scope and to include examples from virtually all of the social sciences. Dozens of dissertations are cited as examples of the wide diversity in topics and methods of inquiry. We have included guidelines for both quantitative and qualitative dissertations and we have solicited and presented suggestions from students who have recently completed their own dissertations.

Throughout we have tried to provide sufficient detail so that the book can serve as a relatively comprehensive reference work for matters of form and content. We appreciate the instructive comments of a number of individuals who reviewed drafts of the manuscript: Lawrence Mohr, University of Michigan; Bruce Thyer, University of Georgia; Bob Greene, Case Western University; Alan Acock, Oregon State University; and Craig Frisby, University of Florida. We are also indebted to Hilde Keldemans, who produced the figures and graphs, and to Leslie Kunkel, who made valuable suggestions re-garding computer-based literature searches.

Special thanks go to C. Deborah Laughton, our continually upbeat editor at Sage, who was an ally from the outset of the project. Our colleagues at The Fielding Institute and California State University Fullerton have been ongoing sources of wisdom and creativity. In particular, we thank Jody Veroff for her humane approach to schol-arly writing, exemplified in her contribution of a chapter to the book. Finally, we cannot envision having completed this project without the help of two groups of individuals: our families, who showed tolerance beyond the bounds of reasonable expectations, and our students, whose own dissertation journeys provided the source ma-terial and inspiration for the book. It is they who consistently have demonstrated that the doctoral dissertation can be a transformative professional and personal experience.

PART 1

Getting Started

1 ✔

The Research Process

████

There is the story of a Zen Buddhist who took a group of monks into the forest, whereupon the group soon lost their way. Presently one of the monks asked their leader where they were going. The wise man answered, "To the deepest, darkest part of the forest, so that we can all find our way out together." Doctoral research for the graduate student in the social sciences is often experienced in just that manner, trekking into a forest of impenetrable density and false turns. Over the years our students have employed various metaphors to describe the dissertation process, metaphors that support the feeling of being lost in the wilderness. One student compared the process to the Sisyphean struggle of reaching the top of a hill, only to discover the presence of an even higher mountain behind it. Another student experienced the task as learning a Martian language, known to the natives who composed her committee but entirely foreign to her. A third student had perhaps the best description when she suggested that it was like waiting patiently in an interminable line to gain admission to a desirable event, finally reaching the front, only to be told to return to the rear of the line!

One reason that students become more exasperated than necessary on the dissertation journey is that they fail to understand the procedures and practices that form the foundation for contemporary social science research. Many students who are attracted to their field of interest out of an applied concern are apprehensive about making the leap from application to theory that is an indispensable part of the research enterprise. What may not be so evident is that many of the skills that go into being a consummate practitioner are the same skills that are demanded in order to become a capable researcher. It is well known that curiosity and hypothesis-testing are the bedrock of empirical research. In a similar fashion, experienced psychotherapists, to take an example from clinical psychology, are sensitive and keen observers of client behavior. They are persistent hypothesis-testers. They are curious about the relationship between family history variables and current functioning. They draw upon theory and experience to help select a particular intervention for a particular client problem or moment in therapy.

Dispassionate logic and clear and organized thinking are as necessary for effectiveness in the field as they are for success in research. In fact, the bridge between research and just plain living is much shorter than most people think. All of us gather data about the world around us, wonder what will happen if we or others behave in particular ways, and test our pet hunches through deliberate action. To a large extent, the formal research enterprise consists of thinking systematically about these same issues.

The procedures outlined in this book are intended to assist the doctoral student in planning and writing a research dissertation. The suggestions are equally applicable to writing a master's thesis. There is considerable overlap between these two challenging activities. For most students the master's thesis is the first rigorous research project they attempt. This means that, in the absence of strong, supportive faculty consultation, the student often concludes the thesis with considerable relief and an awareness of how not to do the study the next time! With a doctoral dissertation, it is generally expected, sometimes as an act of faith, that the student will be a more seasoned and sophisticated researcher. The consensus opinion is that dissertations are generally longer than theses, that they are more original, and that they make a greater contribution to the field.

In most graduate programs the prelude to conducting a dissertation study is presenting a dissertation proposal. A research proposal is an action plan that justifies and describes the proposed study. We take the completion of a comprehensive proposal as a very important step in the dissertation process. The proposal serves as a contract between the student and his or her dissertation or thesis committee that, when approved by all parties, constitutes an agreement that data may be collected and the study may be completed. As long as the student follows the steps outlined in the proposal, committee members should be discouraged from demanding significant changes to the study after

Figure 1.1. The Research Wheel

the proposal has been approved. Naturally, it is not uncommon to expect small changes or additions or deletions down the road, because one can never totally envision the unpredictable turns that studies can take.

There is no universally agreed upon format for the research proposal. By our way of thinking, a good proposal contains a review of the relevant literature, a statement of the problem and the associated hypotheses, and a clear delineation of the proposed method and plans for data analysis. In our experience, an approved proposal means that more than half of the work of the dissertation has been completed. This book is intended to help students construct research proposals as well as completed dissertations.

THE RESEARCH WHEEL

One way of thinking about the phases of the research process is with reference to the so-called research wheel (see Figure 1.1). The wheel metaphor suggests that research is not linear but a recursive cycle of steps that are repeated over time. The most common entry point is some form of "empirical observation." In other words, the researcher selects a topic from the infinite array of possible topics. The next step is a process of inductive logic that culminates in a proposition. The inductive process serves to relate the specific topic to a broader context and begins with some hunches of the form, "I wonder if . . ." These hunches are typically guided by the values, assumptions, and goals of the researcher that need to be explicated.

Stage two of the research wheel is a developed proposition, which is expressed as a statement of an established relationship (e.g., "The early bird is more likely to catch the worm than the late bird"). The proposition exists within a conceptual or theoretical framework. It is the role of the researcher to clarify the relationship between a particular proposition and the broader context of theory and previous research. This is probably the most challenging and creative aspect of the dissertation process. A conceptual framework, which is simply a less developed form of a theory, consists of statements that link abstract concepts (e.g., motivation, role) to empirical data. Theories and conceptual frameworks are developed to account for or describe abstract phenomena that occur under similar conditions. A theory is the language that allows us to move from observation to observation and make sense of similarities and differences. Without placing the study within such a context, the proposed study has a "so what?" quality. This is one of the main objections to the research proposals of novice researchers: The research question may be inherently interesting but ultimately meaningless. For instance, the question, "I wonder if there are more women than men in graduate school today?" is totally banal as a research question unless the answer to the question has conceptual or theoretical implications that are developed within the study. A study may be worthwhile primarily for its practical implications (e.g., Should we start recruiting more men into graduate schools?), but a purely applied study may not be acceptable as a dissertation. Kerlinger (1977, p. 5), author of a highly respected text on research methodology, has noted that "the basic purpose of scientific research is theory." Generally speaking, a research dissertation is expected to contribute to the scholarly literature in a field and not merely solve an applied problem. Thus identifying a conceptual framework for a research study typically involves immersing oneself in the research and theoretical literature of the field.

Having stated our position with regard to the role of theory in dissertation research, it becomes necessary for us to take a step back. As a psychologist and a sociologist, we are most familiar with research conventions within these two disciplines. Other branches of the social sciences have their own standards of what constitutes an acceptable dissertation topic. We have attempted to keep this book as generalizable as possible and to infuse it with examples from other fields. Ultimately, of course, you will need to follow the rules and conventions that pertain to your discipline as well as to your university and department. For example, a few major universities allow a doctoral student to submit a series of published articles as equivalent to a dissertation. Many others encourage studies that consist of secondary data analyses derived from national data bases such as census data or the General Social Survey, or data obtained from a larger study. Some fields, notably social work, education, policy evaluation, and professional psychology, may encourage dissertations that solve applied problems rather than make distinct theoretical contributions. Studies that evaluate the effectiveness of programs or interventions are a case in point because they sometimes contribute little in the way of validating a theory. Political science and economics are examples of fields that are diverse enough to accommodate both theoretically based studies and purely applied studies. Within the subspeciality of international relations, for instance, one could imagine a survey and analysis of security agreements of European nations after the unraveling of the North Atlantic Treaty Organization (NATO) that relies on interviews with foreign policymakers and is largely descriptive and applied. In contrast, a study of the role of a commitment to ideology to the success of political parties in the United States, based on an analysis of historical documents and voting records, might be grounded in a theory of how ideology attracts or alienates the voting public.

Moving forward along the research wheel, the researcher uses deductive reasoning to move from the larger context of theory to generate a specific research question. The research question is the precisely stated form of the researcher's intent, and may be accompanied by one or more specific hypotheses. The first loop is completed as the researcher seeks to discover or collect the data that will serve to answer the research question. The data collection process is essentially another task of empirical observation, which then initiates another round of the research wheel. Generalizations are made on the basis of the particular data that have been observed (inductive process), and the generalizations are tied to a conceptual framework, which then leads to the elucidation of further research questions and implications for additional study.

The kinds of skills called for at the various points of the research wheel are reminiscent of the thoughts about learning presented by Bertram Russell many years ago. Russell noted that there are two primary kinds of knowledge acquisition: knowledge by description and knowledge by acquaintance. Knowledge by description is learning in a passive mode, such as reading a book on how to change the oil in one's car or hearing a lecture on Adam Smith's theory of economics. It is the type of learning that is especially well suited for mastering abstract information. Knowledge by acquaintance, on the other hand, is learning by doing, the kind of skill training that comes from practicing a tennis serve, driving an automobile, and playing with a computer. This is concrete knowledge acquisition, oriented to solving problems. The research process demands both skills. First, there is the clear, logical thinking that pertains to working with concepts and ideas and building theories. It is our impression that many graduate students, particularly those who have experience as practitioners in their fields, are weakest in abstract conceptualization, and honing this skill may be the major challenge of the dissertation. Second, there is the practical application of ideas, including the need systematically to plan a study, collect and analyze data. The ability to focus, problem solve, and make decisions will help bring the study to completion.

2 ✔

Selecting a Suitable Topic

The selection of an appropriate topic is the first major challenge in conducting research. In many academic settings, this task is simplified by working with a faculty mentor who is already familiar with an interesting area of study and may even have defined one or more researchable questions. On the other hand, you may not be blessed with a faculty role model who is actively engaged in research in an area of interest to you. There are no simple rules for selecting a topic of interest, but there are some considerations for making a decision as to appropriateness. It is generally unwise to define something as important as a dissertation topic without first obtaining a broad familiarity with the field. This implies a large amount of exploring the literature and talking with the experts. Without this initial exploration you cannot know the range of possibilities of interesting topics nor have a clear idea of what is already known. Most students obtain their research topics from the loose ends they discover in reading within an area, from an interesting observation they have made ("I notice that men shut up when a beautiful woman enters the room; I wonder what the effect of physical attractiveness is on group process"), or from an applied focus in their lives or professional work ("I have a difficult time treating these alcoholics and want to discover how best to work with them"). Another strategy is to consult with leading scholars in an area of interest and ask them for advice on profitable topics to pursue. Most are happy to talk to and share materials with enthusiastic doctoral students who are obviously familiar with the expert's prior work.

SOME GUIDELINES
FOR TOPIC SELECTION

Here are some guidelines for deciding if a topic is appropriate as a dissertation subject:

1. A topic needs to sustain your interest over a long period of time. A suggested study on learning nonsense syllables under two sets of environmental conditions may sound appealing in its simplicity, but remember Finagle's first law of research: If something can go wrong, it will go wrong! Dissertations usually take at least twice as much time as anticipated and there are few worse fates than slaving hour after hour on a project that you abhor. Remember too that all dissertations are recorded and published with the Library of Congress and you will always be associated with this particular study!

2. At the other extreme, it is wise to avoid a topic that is overly ambitious and overly challenging. Most students want to graduate, preferably within a reasonable period of time. Grandiose dissertations have a way of never being completed and even the best dissertations end up being compromises among your own ambition, the wishes of your committee, and practical circumstances. It is not realistic for a dissertation to say everything there is to say about a particular topic (e.g., the European Common Market) and you need to temper your enthusiasm with pragmatism. As one student put it, "There are two types of dissertations: the great ones and those that are completed!" Sometimes it makes sense to select a research topic on the basis of convenience or workability and use the luxury of the postgraduate years to pursue more esoteric topics of personal interest.

3. We suggest that you avoid topics that may be linked too closely with emotional issues in your own life. It always makes sense to choose a topic that is interesting and personally meaningful. Some students, however, try to use a dissertation to resolve an emotional issue or solve a personal problem. Even if you think you have successfully overcome the personal impact of the death of your child, this is a topic to be avoided. It will necessarily stir up emotional issues that may easily get in the way of completing the dissertation.

4. A related issue is selecting a topic in which you have a personal ax to grind. Remember that conducting research demands ruthless

honesty and objectivity. If you initiate a study to demonstrate that men are no damned good, you will not be able to allow yourself the sober reflections of good research nor acknowledge the possibility that your conclusions may contradict your expectations. It is much better to begin with a hunch ("I've noticed that men don't do very well with housekeeping. I wonder if that has something to do with being pampered as children . . ."), and to regard the research as an adventurous exploration to shed light on this topic than as a polemical exercise to substantiate your point of view.

5. Finally, you need to select a topic that has the potential for you to make an original contribution to the field and allow you to demonstrate your independent mastery of subject and method. In other words, the topic must be worth pursuing. At the very least, the study must generate or help validate theoretical understanding in an area, or, in those fields where applied dissertations are permissible, contribute to the development of professional practice. Some students are put off when they discover that a literature review contains contradictory or puzzling results or explanations for a phenomenon. Such contradictions should not be taken as setbacks and reasons to steer away from a topic, but as opportunities to resolve a mystery. When people disagree or when existing explanations seem inadequate, there is often room for a critical study to be conducted.

FROM INTERESTING IDEA
TO RESEARCH QUESTION

Let us assume that you have identified a general area of research and that your choice has been based on curiosity and may involve resolving a problem, explaining a phenomenon, uncovering a process by which something occurs, demonstrating the truth of a hidden fact, building on or reevaluating other studies, or testing some theory in your field. To know whether or not the topic is important (significant) you must also be familiar with the literature in the area. Later on, we will present a number of suggestions for conducting a good review and assessment of the literature. In the meantime, we have noticed that many students have difficulty transforming an interesting idea into a researchable question and have designed a simple exercise to help in that endeavor.

Researchable questions almost invariably involve the relationship between two or more variables, phenomena, concepts, or ideas. The nature of that relationship may vary. Research studies generally consist of methods to explicate the nature of the relationship. Research in the social sciences rarely consists of explicating a single construct (e.g., "I will look at everything there is to know about the 'imposter phenomenon' ") or a single variable (e.g., voting rates in presidential elections).[1] Even the presence of two variables is apt to be limiting and oftentimes it is only when a third "connecting" variable is invoked that an idea becomes researchable.

An example might help to demonstrate how the introduction of an additional variable can lead to the birth of a promising study. Let us assume that I am interested in how the elderly are perceived by a younger generation. At this level a study would be rather mundane and apt to lead to a "so what?" response. So far it implies asking people what they think of the elderly, perhaps using interviews, or tests, or even behavioral observations. But we really won't learn much about perceptions of the elderly in contemporary society. Introducing a second variable, however, can lead to a set of questions that have promising theoretical (as well as practical) implications: I wonder what the role of the media is in shaping social perceptions of the elderly? I wonder if living with a grandparent makes any difference in how the elderly are viewed? I wonder how specific legislation designed to benefit the elderly has changed our perception of them? I wonder if there is a relationship between how middle-aged adults deal with their aging parents and how they view the elderly? The new variables that were introduced in these potential research questions were, respectively, the slant of the media, presence or absence of grandparent, type of legislation, and treatment of own parents. These variables impart meaning to the research because they offer suggestions as to what accounts for variability in the perception of the elderly.

As an example of generating a research question using three primary variables, let's say that you have inferred that many women lose interest in sexual relations with their husbands after the birth of a child. At this level the proposed study would consist of checking out this hunch by assessing the sexual interest of women (variable 1) before and after childbirth (variable 2). But what would this finding mean? The introduction of a third variable or construct could lead to a much more sophisticated and conceptually meaningful study. An investigator might ask, "I wonder if the husband's involvement in parenting makes a difference? What's the role of his sexual initiative? How about childbirth complications? Father's involvement in the birthing? The length of time they have been married? Time after delivery? Presence of other children in the home?" There is no end to the number of interesting questions that can be raised simply by introducing a mediating variable into the proposed study. This variable would then help to explain the nature of the relationship between the primary variables. In fact, one could brainstorm a whole list of potential third variables that could contribute to a better understanding of the relationship between childbirth and sexuality.

Note that the precise function of the third, or "connecting" variable, will depend upon the logic of the conceptual model underlying the study. In this regard, a distinction can be made between two terms, *mediator* and *moderator*, that have often been used interchangeably (Baron & Kenny, 1986). Strictly speaking, a moderator variable pinpoints the conditions under which an independent variable exerts its effects on a dependent variable; a mediating variable, on the other hand, tries to describe "how" rather than "when" effects will occur by accounting for the relationship between the independent variable (the predictor) and the dependent variable (the criterion). In the health psychology field social support can be regarded as either a moderating variable or a mediating variable (Quittner, Glueckauf, & Jackson, 1990). Conceptualized as a moderator, social support could be seen to exert beneficial effects on health outcomes only under conditions of high stress (i.e., there is a statistical interaction between stress and social support). Conceptualized as a mediator, social support acts as an intervening variable between stress and health outcomes (i.e., there is an indirect relationship between stress and illness). Arguing from this model, some stressful events might encourage traumatized individuals to shun or exhaust their supportive resources or perceive them as unhelpful, leading, in turn, to increased symptoms of anxiety and depression. The nature of the role of mediating variables in the theoretical model can be captured by the path diagram in Table 2.1.

Table 2.1 Path Diagram

stressful event	→	social support	→	health outcomes
independent variable		mediating variable		dependent variable

One single research study is not likely to establish and verify all the important elements of a complex conceptual model. As one of

Figure 2.1. A Model of Antisocial Behavior
SOURCE: Patterson, DeBaryshe, & Ramsey (1989)

our colleagues puts it, you would need a video camera to capture the entire Grand Canyon on film, whereas the dissertation is more like a snapshot, perhaps of a mule and rider descending one small section of the canyon trail. Yet the proposed model can provide a useful context for current and future research studies. Most ambitious research studies rely heavily on just such theoretical models. For example, Gerald Patterson (Patterson, DeBaryshe, & Ramsey, 1989) has for some time been developing and testing a model to explain aggressive and deviant behavior among young males. The model hypothesizes that such antisocial behavior can be causally linked to disrupted parental discipline and poor family management skills. However, the relationship between these two sets of variables is not direct, but mediated by a network of other variables. The process is thought to begin with parents "training" a child to behave aggressively by relying on aversive behaviors in both punishment and negative reinforcement contingencies. The inability of the parents to control coercive exchanges among family members constitutes "training for fighting," which leads, in turn, to aggressive behavior and poor peer relationships. This lack of social skills generalizes to antisocial behavior in the classroom, which makes it next to impossible for the youth to obtain basic academic skills, thus preparing him poorly to cope with life outside school. Ultimately, this leads to high rates of delinquent behavior. An abbreviated summary of the model is shown in Figure 2.1.

Obviously, a researcher is in no position to test the entire model in a single study. Indeed, Patterson and his colleagues have spent many years testing and elaborating the nature of these relationships.

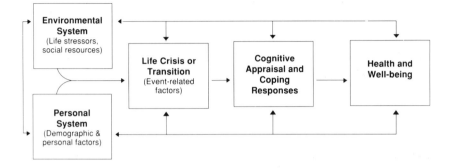

Figure 2.2. A Model of Work Stress and Coping
SOURCE: Moos (1985)

A single study might focus on one particular set of relationships within this complex model. For instance, the investigator might ask whether there is a relationship between physical fighting and poor peer relationships. Each variable would have to be operationalized, probably by obtaining more than one measure of both fighting and peer relationships. In Patterson's work, for instance, he asks mothers, peers, and teachers to rate levels of physical fighting, because their perspectives may differ. Likewise, peers, teachers, and self-report are used to obtain measures of peer relations. The objective of the study, that is, attempting to determine the nature and form of the relationship between the primary variables, will determine the research method that is employed.

A second example of using a comprehensive model as a guide to research comes from Rudolf Moos's (1985) ongoing studies of work and family environments. Basically, Moos has adopted a socio-ecological view of work. The model describes both environmental variables and personal variables and relates them, via a set of cognitive functions and coping variables, to individual adaptation, including morale, job performance, and overall health and well-being (see Figure 2.2). A single study might focus on a small set of environmental system variables and relate them to something else, such as other environmental system variables, personal system variables, coping responses, or health outcomes. For instance, the researcher might explore the contribution of work pressure and supervisory support on innovation in the workplace.

Table 2.2 Brainstorming Exercise

Begin by defining one or two variables (or constructs) of interest. Then generate a list of additional variables (or constructs) that in some way amplify the original variables or illuminate the relationship between them. The new variables you list may be either independent variables, dependent variables, moderating variables, or even mediating variables in the research questions you eventually select. After brainstorming this list, go back and eliminate those variables that do not interest you or do not seem promising to pursue. Finally, see if you can now define one or more research questions that speak to the relationship among the two or three variables (or constructs) you have specified. Ultimately, each of these variables will need to be operationally defined as you develop your research study.

Here are some examples of the results of this brainstorming exercise applied to topics taken from different disciplines:

Political Science

Begin with an interest in citizen participation in city council meetings. List variables or phenomena that might influence, be influenced by, or be related to this variable. A sample research question is: What is the impact of citizen participation in city council meetings on legislative decision making?

citizen participation		legislative decision making
Independent Variable	→	Dependent Variable

Education

Begin with an interest in single mothers on welfare who return to school. List variables or phenomena that might influence, be influenced by, or be related to this variable. A sample research question is: What is the role of the availabilty of child care on single mothers on welfare returning to school?

child care		return to school
Independent Variable	→	Dependent Variable

---

continued

GENERATING RESEARCHABLE QUESTIONS

The exercise that we use to help students generate researchable questions from their interesting ideas is a brainstorming exercise that begins with labeling one or two variables and generating a second and/or third. Brainstorming consists of openly and noncritically listing all possible ideas in a given period of time. Later on you can return to a more critical analysis of each idea and delete those that are either uninteresting, nonmeaningful, or impractical. Ultimately, of course, it is contact with the literature that will determine whether or not a research question is viable, because the literature houses the tradition of scholarly inquiry that goes beyond the limits of your own knowledge.

We suggest that you do the brainstorming exercise in a small group so that the person receiving the consultation merely serves as a scribe

Table 2.2 Continued

Criminal Justice

   Begin with an interest in the relationship between neighborhood crime watch programs and robbery rates. List variables that might influence or amplify the relationship between these two variables. A sample research question is: What is the effect of neighborhood crime watch programs, in both urban and rural environments, on the rate of burglaries?

   crime watch programs   →   rate of burglaries
                              urban/rural environments

   Independent Variable   Moderator Variable   Dependent Variable

Psychology

   Begin with an interest in the relationship between physical attractiveness and self-esteem. List variables that might amplify or influence the relationship between these two variables. A sample research question is: What is the role of body image and physical attractiveness on self-esteem? Another sample research question is: What is the role of body image in mediating the relationship between physical attractiveness and self-esteem?

           body image
           Independent Variable   → self-esteem
           physical attractiveness   Dependent Variable
           Independent Variable

                                   OR

   physical attractiveness   →   body image   →   self-esteem
   Independent Variable   Mediating Variable   Dependent Variable

---

to record the ideas thrown out by the other group members (see Table 2.2). After 5 or 10 minutes it is time to move on to the next person's partially formed research topic. We generally use this exercise in groups of three or four so that group members can frequently shift groups and draw on the spontaneous reactions of a larger number of peers uncontaminated by prior ideas or a particular mind set. The exercise involves suspending critical thinking and allowing new ideas to percolate. It should especially suit divergent thinkers, who will find the demand to be expansive in their thinking to be exciting and creative. Convergent thinkers may experience the exercise as a bit overwhelming, but they will find fulfillment in other stages of the research process that demand compulsivity, care, and precision. Every chapter of a dissertation contains both divergent and convergent elements.

   Note that not all decent research studies focus on three (or more) primary variables. Many studies look at the relationship between two variables or concepts, and a few descriptive studies make do with one variable or construct. This generally occurs in the early

Table 2.3 Outline of Issues for a Student Researcher to Complete in the Development of the Research Proposal

---

Review of the Literature
  The classic, definitive, or most influential pieces of research in this area are:
  The journals that specialize in the kind of research in which I propose to engage are:
  The body(ies) of research to which I wish to add is (are):
  The experts in the field of my research are:
Statement of the Problem
  The intellectual problem(s) I may help solve through this research is (are):
  The moral, political, social, or practical problem(s) I may help alleviate through this
    research is (are):
Method
  The method I propose to use to answer my question, prove my point, or gain more
    detailed and substantive knowledge is:
  An alternative way to do it would be:
  Three important research studies that have been carried out using the method I
    propose are:
  The reason(s) this method is a good one for my question, proposition, or subject is
    (are):
  Possible weaknesses of this method are:
  The skills I will need to use this method are:
  Of these skills I still need to acquire the following:
  I propose to acquire these skills by:

---

stages of research in an area when little is known about a topic. Some investigators are pathfinders in terms of opening up new topics of research by trying to understand as much as possible about a phenomenon and generating more informed hypotheses for others to test in the future. Nonetheless, we believe that most students underestimate what is currently known about most topics and that the most interesting, practical, and theoretically meaningful studies are apt to consider the relationships among several variables.

We conclude this chapter with the outline in Table 2.3, which asks you to look at the kinds of issues that need to be considered and responded to during the course of developing the research proposal. By and large, your dissertation committee will need to be convinced of three things in order to be comfortable with your proposal:

1. Is the question clear and researchable and will the answer to the question extend knowledge in your field of study?
2. Have you located your question within a context of previous study that demonstrates that you have mastered and taken into consideration the relevant background literature?
3. Is the proposed method suitable for exploring your question?

Box 2.1

STUDENT SUGGESTIONS

Over the years our students have provided the most useful suggestions for completing the dissertation. Here are some of the suggestions they have offered to one another that pertain to the earliest stages of developing a dissertation. Other suggestions will be noted at the appropriate places in the following chapters.

1. Start an "idea box," a file box to hold 3 × 5 cards or slips of paper where you can store good ideas for future reference. Use the idea box for noting books and articles to get from the library, good quotes, inspirations for future studies, half-baked notions that might be useful in the future, and so on.
2. Don't even think about doing a dissertation without a word processor!
3. Think of your topic as a large jigsaw puzzle with a piece missing. That is what you want to research, to fill in the gap in your field. To discover what piece is missing, you must read as much of the literature as possible in your field.
4. Before you begin, read several well-written dissertations recommended by your chairperson.
5. As you progress through the dissertation process and your question shrinks in size due to the necessity of maintaining a manageable project for one person, don't lose heart. Even very small questions can serve much larger purposes. To keep the perspective of "meaningfulness" throughout, keep imagining an audience of individuals who would want to know the results of your work. Even if you can only imagine 25 people in the whole world who would care, keep that group alive in front of your eyes.

NOTE

1. A construct is a concept used for scientific purposes in building theories. Constructs (e.g. self-esteem), like concepts, are abstractions formed by generalizing from specific behaviors or manipulations. When constructs are operationalized in such a way that they can be "scored" to take on different numerical values, they are referred to as variables.

3 ✔

Methods of Inquiry: Quantitative and Qualitative Approaches

The principal characteristic of scholarly and scientific inquiry, as opposed to informal, intuitive kinds of inquiry, is the use of rationally grounded procedures to extend knowledge that a community of scholars regards as reliable and valid (Human and Organization Development Knowledge Area Study Guides [HOD], 1991). The dissertation process is a ritual of socialization into that community of scholars, so it is necessary for you, as a student, to master the scholarly procedures within your discipline. The specific methods chosen to attack a problem will depend upon your discipline and the nature of the specific problem. There is no universally accepted approach within the social sciences, although there are rich research traditions that cannot be ignored, as well as a common understanding that chosen methods of inquiry must rest on rational justification. This means that scientific methods differ from more informal methods of inquiry by their reliance on validated public procedures that have been determined to produce reliable knowledge.

Currently there are many disagreements in the social sciences regarding what constitutes knowledge and the procedures for gaining it. One way of thinking about the way in which research generally contributes to the knowledge base of a discipline is by considering the following hierarchy of knowledge, suggested by our colleague Marilyn Freimuth.

Axiologic/Epistemic Level. This is the underlying level of basic world hypotheses that form the foundation for content and method within a field of inquiry. *Epistemology* refers to the study of the nature of knowledge, while *axiology* refers to the study of ethics, values, and aesthetics. Examples of constructs at this level include the explanatory principle of cause-and-effect and the notion of open systems. In many ways the 20th century represents a new "axial shift" (Mahoney, 1990), or turning point in the history of ideas, away from a rational objectivism, which asserts that scientific knowledge is founded on objective empirical truths, and toward the conception of a more relativistic universe and "poststructuralist" epistemologies.

Theoretical Level. This is the level of models and theories. Theories are premises to account for data, such as the FIRO theory of interpersonal behavior in groups (Schutz, 1966) or the differential association theory in the study of crime (Sutherland, 1924). The term *model* has been used in many, often confusing ways in the social sciences, but refers here to a higher order theory, that is, a representational system at a higher level of abstraction that can inform and be informed by alternative theories (close to the framework or worldview that helps guide researchers and has been identified as a "paradigm" by Thomas Kuhn [1962]). Thus, psychoanalysis could be seen as a model, a wide lens by which to view and understand the mysteries of human behavior. Each model carries with it certain sets of assumptions. In the case of psychoanalysis, these assumptions include the unifying importance of causal determinism and unconscious motivation as core constructs.

Empirical Level. In the field of epistemology, *empiricism* refers to a commitment to obtaining knowledge through sense experience (literally, "based on experience" in Greek). Empiricism is frequently contrasted with *rationalism,* which refers to knowledge derived purely through thought and reason, and to more natural philosophical and religious traditions of reaching conclusions. In the present context, the empirical level includes hypotheses and the methods and data of scientific research. Hypotheses are tentative answers to questions generally based on theory.

The primary role of research within this schema is to link the theoretical and the empirical. Theories need the support of data in order to remain viable, while methods themselves carry assumptions that are theoretical in nature. Note that research findings do not contribute directly to the axiologic/epistemic level or even to basic models. Those levels reflect fundamental value commitments and personal preferences that are rarely modified on the basis of additional data, especially the kind of data generated by scholarly research. It is hard to imagine a psychoanalyst becoming a behaviorist or a Republican joining the Democrats without a significant shift in values that goes beyond the accumulated wisdom imparted by a series of research studies. Because most researchers strongly identify with particular values and carry many personal preferences into their work, it becomes especially important to learn to discriminate between beliefs and opinions, on the one hand, and verifiable, data-inspired support for ideas, on the other hand.

A brief look at the history of science is a humbling experience that should put to rest the misguided notion that research discovers truth. Drilling holes in the skull (trephining) used to be an acceptable way of dismissing the demons responsible for mental illness and it wasn't that long ago that the sun was thought to circle the earth. One wonders what remnants of contemporary scientific truth will be regarded as equally ludicrous tomorrow! Instead, what research does contribute is a series of thoughtful observations that support or question the validity of our theories, which are in turn based on a set of largely untestable beliefs and assumptions. And every once in a while, at opportunistic moments of scholarly upheaval, a new paradigm appears that seems to do a better job of explaining the available data and guiding further inquiry.

Each social science discipline and set of investigators seems to have its own favored approach to generating knowledge. For instance, public opinion studies usually rely on survey research methods, psychoanalytic studies of infants make use of observational techniques, studies of organizational effectiveness may employ action research methods and case studies, historical investigations of political and social events rely on archival records and content analysis, and laboratory studies of perceptual processes stress experimental manipulation and hypothesis testing. Within your chosen field, it is important to ask how a piece of research acquires legitimacy as reliable knowledge (HOD, 1991). No doubt part of the answer comes down to underlying epistemological assumptions and values. Certainly research strategies will differ in terms of the problems they address and the outcomes they produce. As we shall see, one important distinction in the choice of method seems to be the nature of the relationship between the researcher and the topic of study.

We would argue that researchers in the social sciences have generally been myopic in defining the kinds of studies that might legitimately lend themselves to research dissertations. Most students in the social sciences are taught early on about the difference between independent and dependent variables and how experimental research implies active manipulation of independent variables to observe a subsequent impact on dependent variables. This basic and time-honored strategy has an earthy history in the systematic evaluation of fertilizers for agricultural productivity. It remains a cornerstone in conducting social science research with human subjects. Yet it is certainly not the only way to conduct research.

The only universal in scientific knowledge is a general commitment to using logical argument and evidence to arrive at conclusions that are recognized as tentative and subject to further amendment (HOD, 1991). Good scientists in action often deviate from an "official" philosophy of science and a prescribed methodology. As William Bevan (1991) has recently noted,

> if you want to understand what effective science making is about, don't listen to what creative scientists say about their formal belief systems. Watch what they do. When they engage in good, effective science making they don't, as a rule, reflect on their presuppositions; they engage in a practical art form in which their decisions are motivated by the requirements of particular problem solving.(p. 478)

The key to evaluating a completed study is whether or not the selected method is sufficiently rigorous and appropriate to the research question, and whether or not the study is conceptually and theoretically grounded. The more familiar you are with the full range of alternative research strategies, the more enlightened and appropriate the choice of a particular method is apt to be. Too often students become so enamored with an approach to research that they will choose the method prior to determining the question. Unless the dissertation is designed to illustrate the use of a promising and innovative methodology, this is getting the cart before the horse. In general, the method needs to evolve out of the research question and be determined by it.

QUANTITATIVE METHODS

The epistemological foundation of most social science inquiry in the 20th century has been logical positivism, a school of thought that maintains that all knowledge is derived from direct observation and logical inferences based on direct observation. To a great extent, the notion of objectively studying human beings is derived from a love affair social scientists have had with the natural sciences, which sought to understand nature by isolating phenomena, observing them, and formulating mathematical laws to describe patterns in nature. Current research in the social sciences is very steeped in the empirical and quantitative traditions.

Statistical methods are especially useful for looking at relationships and patterns and expressing these patterns with numbers. Descriptive statistics describe these patterns of behavior, while inferential statistics use probabilistic arguments to generalize findings from samples to populations of interest. Kerlinger (1979) focuses on the inferential process when he defines *statistics* as, "the theory and method of analyzing quantitative data obtained from samples of observations in order to study and compare sources of variance of phenomena, to help make decisions to accept or reject hypothesized relations between the phenomena, and to aid in making reliable inferences from empirical observations" (p. 185). Note that the focus in the natural science model of research is the study of average or group effects as opposed to the study of individual differences. The kinds of inferential statements that derive from this model of research refer to groups of people or groups of events, that is, they are probabilistic (e.g., "Surveys find that most people believe that police officers use excessive force in dealing with criminals" or "Emotional expressiveness is related to coping effectively with natural disasters").

In experimental research, quantitative research designs are used to determine aggregate differences between groups or classes of subjects. Emphasis is placed on precise measurement and controlling for extraneous sources of error. The purpose, therefore, is to isolate a variable of interest (the independent variable) and manipulate it to observe the impact of the manipulation on a second, or dependent, variable. This procedure is facilitated by the "control" of extraneous variables, thus allowing the researcher to infer a causal relationship between the two (or more) variables of interest.

Methodological control is generally accomplished by two procedures that rely on the principle of randomness. One is *random sampling,* using subjects that have "randomly" been drawn from the potential pool of subjects so that each member of the population has an equal chance of being selected. Random selection of subjects permits the researcher to generalize the results of the study from the sample to the population in question. The second procedure is *random-*

ization, assigning subjects to groups or experimental conditions in such a way that each subject has an equal chance of being selected for each condition. Subject characteristics are thus randomly distributed in every respect other than the experimental manipulation or treatment, allowing the researcher to infer that resultant differences between the groups must be due to the isolated variable in question.

Unfortunately, these efforts at experimental control are often impractical in social science research with human subjects. Psychology, for instance, has an honorable tradition of laboratory research using tight experimental designs, but research in the clinical or social arena may not permit the kind of control stipulated by the experimental method. This dilemma is equally prominent in field studies in the disciplines of sociology, education, and political science. One cannot practically conspire to rear children using two distinct parenting styles, nor ethically proceed to instill child abuse to study its immediate impact in a controlled fashion. Researchers can, however, study analogues of these variables using pure experimental designs (for example, one can ask parents to use specific interventions at the onset of particular child behaviors). Change studies, in which a treatment or program is being evaluated for its effectiveness, may also lend themselves well to experimental designs. Even so, it may not be possible to randomize subjects into groups that receive a treatment or intervention and those that do not. A number of ingenious solutions have been proposed to deal with the ethics of denying treatment to the needy, including the use of placebos and waiting-list controls (Kazdin, 1992).

More typically, the research method of choice in the social sciences seems to be a "quasi-experimental" design that compromises some of the rigor of the controlled experiment, but maintains the argument and logic of experimental research (Cook & Campbell, 1979). This kind of research has also been called "ex post facto research," a systematic empirical approach in which the investigator does not employ experimental manipulation nor random assignment of subjects to conditions because events have already occurred or they are inherently not manipulable (Kerlinger, 1979). So-called causal statements become correlational statements in quasi-experimental research, although it is often possible to infer a sequence of events in causal form. That is one reason why it is crucial to have a theoretical model as a foundation for an empirical study. The model itself will help to inform you in meaningfully interpreting the results of the study.

There is also a need to exercise caution in interpreting the meaning of results whenever subjects assign themselves to groups. A colorful example is the apparent negative correlation that exists between the numbers of mules found in the various states and the number of Ph.D.s living there. The fact that states that have a lot of mules don't have so many Ph.D.s, and vice-versa, is an empirical observation that can be statistically expressed in the form of a correlation coefficient. A researcher would be hard pressed to argue a causal relationship between these two variables unless she drew upon an underlying theoretical model that links the two variables through a third (mediating) variable such as the degree of urbanization. Note that this simple correlational study could, at least theoretically, be transformed into an experimental study by, for example, flooding some states with mules to see if the Ph.D.s leave or wooing the Ph.D.s across state lines to see if the number of mules increases!

This is not a book on research design, but the adoption of a particular research strategy will affect the final form of the dissertation. Whether or not a study employs a true experimental design or a quasi-experimental design, the most common strategy in the social sciences is a comparison between groups. That is, independent groups of subjects are used for each experimental or control condition. The best known variant of this strategy is to use two equivalent groups of subjects, both of which receive pretests and posttests and differ only in the experimental treatment that is given to one group (see Table 3.1).

Table 3.1 Pretest, Posttest, Control Group Design

	Pretest	Treatment	Posttest
Experimental	yes	yes	yes
Control	yes	no	yes

It becomes possible to evaluate the impact of an intervention because the control group offers a baseline for comparison. One could use this design to evaluate, for example, whether the inclusion of spouses in an aftercare program for heart bypass surgery patients will encourage greater compliance with medical regimens. Or one could design a study to evaluate the effect of introducing air bags in automobiles on the rate of physical injury to passengers. Some automobiles of a given make would receive air bags, some would not, and the change in types and rates of injuries would be the dependent measure.

The straightforward pretest, posttest control group design makes it possible to attribute the impact of experimental interventions to the interventions themselves rather than to some extraneous variable. The interpretation of results of studies using this design may, however, be compromised if the subjects have not been assigned to conditions in a truly random manner. In the proposed "air bag" study, for example, if automobiles and drivers are not randomly assigned to conditions, it may well be that inherently safer drivers will choose automobiles with better safety features. Because randomization is not always possible, it becomes crucial to argue for the "equivalence" of the two groups even if they do not derive from the identical population of subjects. One way in which researchers attempt to make this argument is by matching the groups on key variables that are critical to the understanding of the study, such as age, sex, symptomatology, or, in the current example, the previous driving records of the participants.

The basic pretest, posttest, control group design, shown above, also does not adequately control for any effect that the pretest evaluations might themselves have on the subjects. Some assessments can sensitize subjects by making them aware that they are now participating in a study or providing a practice experience that contaminates the validity of posttest results. A simple posttest only design may get around this difficulty and is probably underutilized in the literature (Campbell & Stanley, 1966). In any case, the choice of a basic research design does not eliminate the need for you to think carefully and creatively about potential sources of error and alternative explanations to account for findings.

Most experimental designs are variants of the treatment and control group format described above.[1] Such designs permit the researcher to make causal inferences regarding the relationships among the variables. In contrast, correlational (or "observational") studies do not generally enable the researcher to demonstrate causal relationships among variables. Any conclusions regarding causality must be inferred from the underlying theory rather than from the results of the study itself.

Studies built around experimental or correlational designs generate data that are subsequently analyzed using appropriate inferential statistics. Statistical techniques that are used to evaluate the effectiveness of an intervention or a difference between groups, such as an Analysis of Variance (ANOVA) or t test, compare the size of "between-group" differences with the size of "within-group" differences due to individual variability. They represent the experimental tradition. The logic of the correlational paradigm is quite different (Cronbach, 1975). Correlations depend upon comparing two distributions of scores, that is, scores that are broadly dispersed along two dimensions, such as longevity and alcohol use. Statistical techniques that emerged from this tradition, such as multiple regression, are especially popular in social science research that relies on questionnaires, surveys, or scales, and the relationship between continuous variables. Be aware, however, that it is the design of the study and not the choice of statistical method that principally governs the types of statements that can be made about the relationships among the variables.

Both experimental and correlational traditions have a rightful place in the evaluation of quantitative data and a detailed comparison of them goes beyond the scope of this book. It is important to remember that although statistics is an indispensable tool for scientific inference, the appropriate application of statistics cannot make up for a faulty research design. In many instances statistical methods drawn from both the experimental and correlational paradigms are equally legitimate choices (cf. Gigerenzer, 1991). As a matter of fact, the same data can usually be analyzed in multiple ways. If you are looking at the relationship between locus of control and frequency of medical visits for preventive health, for example, you could express it using a correlation coefficient or by dividing your sample into two or more subgroups on the basis of the personality construct of locus of control and comparing the resulting groups on medical visits. Generally speaking, it is not a good idea to throw away data (you are throwing away data if you have a continuum of locus of control scores but arbitrarily reduce the continuum to two or more discrete values, such as internal or external categories), but these kinds of decisions require statistical expertise and theoretical grounding.

There are two additional points we wish to make regarding the use of quantitative research. One is that there is a tendency in the social sciences to overemphasize the importance of "statistically significant" findings and to underemphasize the importance of clinically or socially significant findings. In other words, simply because a difference is significant at a certain probability level (typically .05 or .01) does not mean that the difference will be meaningful in practical terms. For instance, a difference of five points on a depression scale might be statistically meaningful, but may not be meaningful clinically. Too often students will assume that the object of research is to achieve statistical significance rather than to make meaningful inferences about behavior. The primary reason that Jacob Cohen (1990), the father of power analysis, was drawn to correlational analyses is that they yield an r, a measure of effect size. That is, unlike probability (p) values, correlation coefficients can straightforwardly indicate the magnitude of the relationship between variables, which may be far more informative than the presence or absence of statistical significance. Cohen (1990) goes on to note that we sometimes learn more from what we see than from what we compute, and argues for an increased use of the graphic display of data, using simple scatter plots and so-called stem and leaf diagrams (see Table 3.2) prior to or instead of performing complicated statistical analyses.

Second, as you consider the kinds of designs and controls that are available to the social science researcher, we urge you to be aware of a fundamental dilemma. Good research is a constant balancing act between control and meaningfulness. At the one extreme is an emphasis on controlling the observation and measurement of a variable by eliminating the influence of as many confounding variables as possible. What results might be a tight laboratory study in which the findings inspire confidence but are not particularly interesting. At the other extreme is the observation of complex human behavior in the field, without invoking any controls at all, so that the results seem fascinating but are highly unreliable and difficult to replicate. The fashion in social science research has moved back and forth between these poles of emphasizing precision of measurement versus emphasizing meaningfulness. Today the pendulum seems to be swinging in the direction of meaningfulness, hastened by the availability of a greater number of permissible research strategies together with a reevaluation of research epistemology.

QUALITATIVE METHODS

The researcher who employs experimental and quasi-experimental designs attempts to control the playing field of the study as much as possible, restrict the focus of attention to a relatively narrow band of behavior (often manipulating experimental conditions in order to further narrow the object of study to a single variable), and get out of harm's way as a detached and objective observer of the action. A countervailing trend in social science research calls for sidestepping the artificiality and narrowness of experimental studies by promoting studies that allow researchers to be more spontaneous and flexible in exploring phenomena in their natural environment. Some of these methods of inquiry are challenging the epistemological and philosophical foundations of traditional social science research (cf. Guba & Lincoln, 1981; Patton, 1980; Spradley, 1979). At one extreme,

Table 3.2 Stem and Leaf Displays

A new graphic display for presenting the distribution of continuously scaled data is the stem and leaf display. A stem and leaf display presents the data in a manner that highlights characteristics of the distribution that might not be obvious from an examination of the frequency distribution. For example, the table below presents the frequencies of age at first marriage for a sample of 91 U.S. residents selected from the National Opinion Research Center General Social Survey of 1990.

Age at First Marriage	f	Age at First Marriage	f
15	1	26	4
16	2	27	4
17	5	28	2
18	8	29	1
19	10	30	2
20	10	31	1
21	12	32	1
22	8	33	1
23	6	34	0
24	6	35	1
25	5	36	1
		Total	91

In a stem and leaf display the first digit of the variable is broken away from the second digit. The first digit forms a "stem" and the second a "leaf." The stem is placed to the left of a vertical line and the leaf is placed to the right. In the age at first marriage data the stems are "10s" and the leaves are "1s." Thus, a person married at 21 would be represented by a 2 stem and a 1 leaf. A person married at 25 would also be represented by the 2 stem, but would have a 5 leaf.

The steps in constructing a stem and leaf display from the above data would be first to select the stems from the above frequency distribution, as follows:

Stems

1

2

3

Then add leaves for each case by observing its second digit and adding that digit to the stem to form the leaf. Thus, in this display, each case is represented by one leaf:

Stems	*Leaves*
1	5667777788888888999999999
2	000000000011111111111122222222233333334444445555566667777889
3	0012356

When working with data that are not ordered, the leaves can be added and then ordered in a final step. The above figure indicates that most persons in this sample were married in their early twenties or late teens. Though there is nothing particularly surprising about this, more complex displays can present a large amount of data in an efficient and descriptive figure that allows the reader to view the distribution in a manner that a simple frequency table does not. Chapter 2 of Hamilton's (1990) *Modern Data Analysis* presents detailed instructions on the construction of complex stem and leaf displays.

proponents of alternative approaches question the validity of a logical positivistic science applied to human behavior and social systems and take issue with the ideal or even the possibility of having a neutral, disengaged investigator (cf. Feyerabend, 1981a, 1981b; Popper, 1965; Toulmin, 1972). Taking their hint from modern physics, they suggest that the presence of an observer inevitably alters that which is being observed, that, in fact, one cannot separate the investigator from the object of inquiry. Feminist theorists have other reasons for criticizing the traditional experimental method, claiming that it creates a hierarchy of power in which the omnipotent researcher, often a male, instructs, observes, records, and sometimes deceives the subjects (Peplau & Conrad, 1989). It should be noted, however, that whether a study uses experimental or nonexperimental methods does not necessarily imply anything about the researcher's commitment to nonsexist research.

The impact of these developments in the philosophy of science upon method is far from clear. We are probably experiencing just the initial foray into the application of alternate research paradigms to the pursuit of research itself. Because a thrust of this book is to advise the use of the most appropriate method for the study of a particular research question, it might be useful to describe briefly some of the distinctions among the various alternative methods. The labels given to these approaches include "phenomenological," "hermeneutic," "naturalistic," "experiential," "dialectical," and so on. The label most commonly used to incorporate these research strategies is "qualitative research." *Qualitative* implies that the data are in the form of words as opposed to numbers. Whereas quantitative data are generally evaluated using descriptive and inferential statistics, qualitative data are usually reduced to themes or categories and evaluated subjectively. There is more emphasis on description and discovery and less emphasis on hypothesis testing and verification. According to Polkinghorne (1991, p. 112), qualitative methods are especially useful in the "generation of categories for understanding human phenomena and the investigation of the interpretation and meaning that people give to events they experience." Piaget's theory of cognitive development, for instance, was developed using qualitative methods. Whereas the quantitative researcher is apt to record a small set of previously identified variables, the qualitative researcher seeks a psychologically rich, indepth understanding of the individual, and would argue that experimental and quasi-experimental methods cannot do justice to describing phenomena such as the therapeutic relationship or the experience of the homeless (Searight, 1990).

Although there exists great heterogeneity within the literature on qualitative methodologies, it is probably fair to say that all such methods share three fundamental assumptions (Patton, 1980):

A Holistic View. The holistic approach stresses that the whole is greater than the sum of its parts. Consequently, qualitative methods seek to understand phenomena in their entirety in order to develop a complete understanding of a person, program, or situation. This is in contrast to the experimental paradigm, which aims to isolate and measure narrowly defined variables, and where understanding is tantamount to prediction and control.

An Inductive Approach. Qualitative research begins with specific observations and moves toward the development of general patterns that emerge from the cases under study. The researcher does not impose much of an organizing structure or make assumptions about the interrelationships among the data prior to making the observations. This is, of course, quite different from the hypothetico-deductive approach to experimental designs that prescribe specification of variables and hypotheses prior to data collection.

Naturalistic Inquiry. Qualitative research is intended to understand phenomena in their naturally occurring states. It is a discovery-oriented approach in the natural environment. Experimental research, by comparison, uses controlled conditions and a limited set of outcome variables.

The appropriate selection of methods of inquiry is contextual and depends to a large extent upon learning the standards used in your own discipline. Qualitative methods have an especially comfortable home in the ethnographic and field study traditions of anthropology and sociology that emerged in the 19th century. Psychologists and psychiatrists also developed detailed case histories of their patients at about that time. Any classification of qualitative methods today is apt to be a simplification. Three dimensions that seem important in contrasting the various qualitative research traditions are (a) the problems and concerns of the researcher, (b) the nature of knowledge, and (c) the relationship between the researcher and the subject matter. These dimensions are summarized in relation to the research traditions of phenomenology, hermeneutics, and ethnographic inquiry in Table 3.3.

PHENOMENOLOGY

When phenomenology is applied to research the focus is on what the person experiences in a language that is as loyal to the lived experience as possible (Polkinghorne, 1989). Thus phenomenological inquiry attempts to describe and elucidate the meanings of human experience. More than other forms of inquiry, phenomenology attempts to get beneath how people describe their experience to the structures that underlie consciousness. Phenomenologically oriented researchers typically use interviews or extended conversations as the source of their data. Important skills for the researcher include listening, observing, and forming an empathic alliance with the subject. The investigator remains watchful of themes that are presented, but resists any temptation to structure or analyze the meanings of an observation prematurely. Once the basic observations are recorded the data may be reduced, reconstructed, and analyzed as a public document.

Several of our doctoral students have developed dissertations based on qualitative interviews. In one study, a student interviewed families shortly after a reunion with an adult member who had been released from prison (Wardell, 1985). The object of the interviews was to get as close as possible to the experience of the transition between prison and family life. In another study a doctoral student interviewed young women who had previously given up children for adoption in an effort to understand the relationship between the adoption process and female adolescent development (Monserrat, 1989). A third student sought to learn about the "coming out" experience of lesbian women by interviewing women who had had both heterosexual and homosexual relationships (Kranzberg, 1988).

HERMENEUTICS

Hermeneutics has been described as the interpretation of texts or transcribed meanings (Polkinghorne, 1983). One engages in a hermeneutic approach to data in order to derive a better understanding of the context that gives it meaning. Hermeneutics, as a specialized field of study, was pioneered by biblical scholars who used textual analysis and interpretation to elicit the meaning of religious text. More recently, researchers in the social sciences have extended the application of hermeneutics to the interpretation of secular texts. Apparently there is ongoing debate within the field of hermeneutics

Table 3.3 Qualitative Research Traditions

Phenomenology

    Problems and concerns of the researcher: Concerned with describing the lived experience of the person as free as possible from theoretical or social constructs. Concerned with accessing the meaning of human phenomena as expressed through the individual.

    Nature of knowledge: Not interested in explanation (What causes X?) but with "What *is* X?" Interested in the essential features of experience or consciousness.

    Relationship between researcher and subject matter: Researcher is co-creator of the narrative, generated typically through interviewing.

Hermeneutics

    Problems and concerns: Concerned with deriving a rich understanding of the context for data, the setting out of which it arises, and that gives it meaning.

    Nature of knowledge: An openly dialogic process of returning again and again to the object of the inquiry (the text), each time with an increased understanding and a more complete interpretation.

    Relationship between researcher and subject matter: Researchers are very involved in the explanatory process, which intrudes into the context of the data.

Ethnographic Inquiry

    Problems and concerns: Concerned with capturing, interpreting, and explaining the way in which people in a group, organization, community, or society live, experience, and make sense out of their lives, their world, and their society or group.

    Nature of knowledge: May use description, interpretation, and explanation and be inductive (descriptive and interpretive) or deductive (working from theory)

    Relationship between researcher and subject matter: The researcher must have maximal detachment while also being immersed in the subject matter and living it. Takes nothing for granted.

NOTE: This table is adapted from the *Inquiry and Research Knowledge Area Study Guide of the Human and Organizational Development Program of The Fielding Institute* (HOD, 1990).

between the "objectivists," who consider the text to contain meaning independent of the interpreter, and others who view active interpretation as primary to all understanding, a position quite similar to modern constructivist thinking in the philosophy of science (Winograd & Flores, 1986). From this latter orientation, understanding is the fusion of the perspective of the phenomenon and the perspective of the interpreter. All of us bring life experiences and expectations to the task of interpretation, but because even our understanding of ourselves is limited and only partially expressible, interaction with the meaning of the text can help produce a deeper understanding of both observer and the observed. As Mahoney (1990, p. 93) puts it,

"New or changed meanings arise from the active encounter of the text and its reader."

Texts from ancient cultures, for instance, may be analyzed in their historical context with the notion of applying their meanings to current issues. This understanding, which must show the meaning of a phenomenon in a way that is both comprehensible to the research consumer and loyal to the frame of reference of the subject, may then lead to more formal research questions. This is a bit different from the task of phenomenological inquiry. In hermeneutics the data are pregiven to the researcher, while in a standard phenomenological study the researcher helps to create the transcribed narrative that has usually been obtained by interviewing the participant-subject(s) (Hoshmand, 1989).

The hermeneutic approach to research is quite complex. It demands frequent return to the source of data, setting up a dialogue with it, so to speak, asking what it means to the creator of it and trying to integrate that with its meaning to the researcher (HOD, 1991). Consequently, although we are all hermeneutically inclined whenever we seek to learn the contexts of things, ideas, and feelings, hermeneutic inquiry is relatively rare as a formal approach to research in the social sciences. Ambitious, well-known examples of the hermeneutic method are psychodynamically guided biographies, such as Erik Erikson's *Young Man Luther*, and the work of Carl Jung, who used an archetypal, mythic perspective to describe contemporary problems.

A different kind of hermeneutic inquiry is represented by Martin Packer's (1985) interpretive study of moral conflicts between young adults using video recordings. From Packer's perspective, the hermeneutic approach is applicable to the study of all human action, where the action is treated as though it has a "textual" structure. The investigator studies what people do when they are engaged in everyday, practical activities. What sets hermeneutics apart from more empirical or rational orientations is the belief that a particular activity can only be understood in conjunction with understanding the context in which it occurs rather than as an abstraction or a set of causal relationships. As Packer puts it, "The difference between a rationalist or empiricist explanation and a hermeneutic interpretation is a little like the difference between a map of a city and an account of that city by someone who lives in it and walks its streets" (1985, p. 1091). The mapmaker's product is formal and abstract; the inhabitant's map is personal and biased.

ETHNOGRAPHIC INQUIRY

The naturalistic-ethnographic paradigm includes anthropological descriptions, naturalistic research, field research, and participant observations (Hoshmand, 1989). Ethnographers attempt to capture and understand specific aspects of the life of a particular group. The focus is on obtaining full and detailed descriptions from informants.

Ethnographic inquiry can be found on a continuum ranging from relatively pure description to more theoretically guided explanations of cultural, social, and organizational life (HOD, 1991). On the more inductive end of the continuum, the researcher develops theory out of the descriptive and interpretive process; on the deductive end of the continuum, the researcher builds a study out of an established theoretical framework.

Typically, the ethnographer initiates prolonged contact and immersion in a setting of interest while at the same time maintaining as much detachment as possible from the subject matter. The naturalistic setting could be the mental hospital explored in the work of Erving Goffman (1961) or the street corner populated by juvenile gangs. A more traditional anthropological example would be a study of health practices among Native Americans living on a reservation. The investigator might obtain some preliminary understanding of the history of the culture by referring to archival records in preparation for living among the informants for several months. During that time the researcher would keep field notes of all observations and interactions and perhaps follow up the observations with intensive, qualitative interviews. The data are recorded verbatim if possible, using the language of the participant.

Obviously, the data that emerge from this research strategy must be reduced in some way in order to be meaningfully communicated in a dissertation. One method for analyzing such data is called the constant comparative method (Glaser & Strauss, 1967). Data are systematically coded into as many themes and meaning categories as possible. As the categories emerge and are refined, the researcher begins to consider how they relate to one another and what the theoretical implications are. Gradually the theoretical properties of the meaning categories crystallize and form a pattern. The pattern that emerges is sometimes called "grounded theory." The constant comparative method can be seen in many qualitative studies in the social sciences, including research on the client experience of psychotherapy (Rennie, Phillips, & Quartaro, 1988) and in a recent study by one of our students on the yearning of older women to have a child (Rasche, 1991).

DISSERTATION IMPLICATIONS
OF QUALITATIVE RESEARCH

The distinctiveness of qualitative research has implications for the write-up of the research proposal and dissertation. Qualitative research designs are typically not intended to prove or test a theory, and it is more likely that the theory will emerge once the data are collected (an inductive approach rather than a traditional deductive approach). This does not mean, however, that the researcher can ignore the theoretical perspectives of previous work cited in the literature review. We are in general agreement with Miles and Huberman (1984), who take a moderate position on the role of theory in naturalistic studies. They view a conceptual framework as the "current version of the researcher's map of the territory being investigated" (1984, p. 33). This means that the framework may change as the study evolves. The amount of prestructuring will depend upon what is known from the literature about the phenomenon being studied, the measures or instruments that are available, and the time allotted for the study. Very loose designs imply the collection of great amounts of data that may initially look important but turn out to be tangential or irrelevant and great amounts of time to sift through them. At the very least, a conceptual framework allows different investigators who are exploring a similar phenomenon to communicate with one another and compare experiences and results.

Adopting a tentative conceptual framework allows the researcher to bound the study with regard to who and what will and will not be studied. Miles and Huberman (1984) choose to express their conceptual frameworks in terms of graphic "bins" that consist of labels for (1) events, (2) settings, (3) processes, and (4) theoretical constructs. They reason that the researcher will come to the study with some ideas about the content of these bins. For instance, a qualitative study on prison behavior could reflect working decisions focusing on current behavior rather than prior history (events), high security prisons (settings), interactions among prisoners and between prisoners and guards (processes), and authority relations and organizational norms (theoretical constructs). These choices and distinctions are, of course, informed by the theoretical and empirical literature.

Research questions can then be formulated as a way of explicating any theoretical assumptions and orienting the investigator (and the student's committee) to the primary goals and tasks of the study. One cannot study every aspect of prison life—the issues adopted by the researcher and expressed as research questions have direct implications for the choice of methodology. A focus such as, "How prisoners and guards negotiate conflict and express power in relationships" has implications for the behavioral events that will be sampled and the research tools that will be used to obtain information (e.g., field notes, interview transcripts, diaries, prison documents, etc.). Research questions in qualitative research can be revised or reformulated as the study proceeds.

Students selecting a qualitative design need to convince their committees that they understand the role of the qualitative researcher. This includes experience with the sensitive kind of interviewing found in naturalistic studies, whereby the investigator enters the world of the participant subject without a fixed agenda and maintains sufficient scientific rigor in the process. Because the researcher is regarded as a person who comes to the scene with his or her own operative reality, rather than as a totally detached scientific observer, it becomes vital to understand, acknowledge, and share one's own underlying values, assumptions, and expectations. This perspective should become clear in the Review of the Literature and Method chapters of the dissertation. Moreover, researcher subjectivity can be reduced by a variety of data handling procedures. Will there be audio or videotaping to augment written field notes? How will these materials be reduced in scope? Will process notes be included that describe the researcher's reactions at various points of the study? How about the use of pilot studies to test the suitability of procedures? Specification of these ingredients can be convincing documentation to the rigor of the proposed study without compromising the necessary "open contract" of the proposal.

In traditional empirical research we are mindful of the importance of reliability, internal validity, and external validity of measures and procedures. The corresponding terms in naturalistic inquiry are "auditability," "credibility," and "fittingness" (Guba & Lincoln, 1981):

1. *Reliability* concerns the replication of the study under similar circumstances. The naturalistic investigator derives consistency through coding the raw data in ways so that another person could understand the themes and arrive at similar conclusions. The researcher's coding scheme needs to be introduced in the Method chapter, with the understanding that the analysis is apt to be modified both during and after data collection.

2. *Internal validity* refers to the validity of a causal inference. In naturalistic inquiry credibility or truth value is ascertained through

structural corroboration. Such corroboration might be accomplished by spending sufficient time with subjects to check for distortions (prolonged engagement), exploring the participant's experience in sufficient detail (persistent observation), and checking multiple sources of data such as other investigators, written records, diaries, field notes, and so on (triangulation). Peer debriefing, revising working hypotheses as more data become available, clarifying tentative findings with the participants, and videotaping interviews for comparisons with the recorded data are typical procedures for adding to the credibility of the study. These activities would need to be noted in the Method chapter.

3. *External validity* refers to the generalizability of the findings of the study. The qualitative study emphasizes the "thick description" of a relatively small number of subjects within the context of a specific setting. Samples can change as the study proceeds, but generalizations to other subjects and situations are always modest and mindful of the context of individual lives.

Because qualitative data may consist of detailed descriptions of events, situations, and behaviors, as well as direct quotations from people about their experiences and beliefs, the Results chapter of the dissertation will be directly influenced as well. We have found that students often have the mistaken belief that a qualitative study might be easier to conduct, because there are no specific hypotheses and no statistical tests to perform. However, the sifting and resifting of huge amounts of transcripts or open-ended responses into a coherent pattern generally takes as much effort and leads to as much frustration as the statistics that were being avoided. Good research is always taxing in some way.

OTHER POSSIBLE APPROACHES TO DISSERTATIONS

In our experience a combination of quantitative and qualitative methodologies is often a good choice of method. An example is an innovative study by Mary Gergen (1988) on the way in which women think about menopause. Gergen held a "research event" at her home and invited several women there to complete questionnaires that addressed attitudes toward menopause, followed by a group discussion on the topic. The research report combines a quantitative analysis of the responses to the questionnaire with a qualitative analysis of themes generated by the discussion. An analogous approach was used by one of our doctoral students who sought to understand what makes extreme, high-risk athletes engage in what laypersons view as self-destructive behavior (Slanger, 1991). The resulting dissertation combined the objectivity of validated measures of sensation-seeking and perceived competence with open-ended interviews. A final example from another field would be an analysis of the effect of timber dislocation on a logging community by quantitatively assessing the economic impact and qualitatively assessing the emotional impact on families in the community.

Another possible approach to writing a dissertation is to write a *theoretical dissertation* and bypass the need for data collection entirely. This is by no means an easy alternative. Original theoretical contributions are a profound intellectual challenge. One way of describing the difference between a knowledge of the literature required for a standard quantitative or qualitative study and for a theoretical study is by referring to the difference between being a native of a foreign country and a tourist in that country. As a tourist in a foreign environment it might be necessary to learn as much as possible about the country by studying maps, reviewing the customs, and learning the language, but chances are you will never master the country as well as the native speaker. It's the same with research. If you know an area of inquiry inside-out and are intimately familiar with the issues and controversies in the field, you have the chance to contribute a new theory; if you are beginning to review an area of interest to formulate a study, you are probably better off with an empirical study. Of course, most doctoral dissertations have theoretical implications and the data you gather and analyze may create the opening for a brand new way of thinking in the field. That, however, is quite different from starting with the expectation of creating a new theory of consciousness or, a bit more modestly, a revised theory of short-term memory.

If you do choose to pursue a theoretical dissertation, you will be expected to argue from the literature that there is a different way of understanding a phenomenon than has heretofore been presented. Some of the more viable theoretical dissertations in the social sciences are those that bring together or integrate two previously distinct areas. For instance, one of our graduate students was of the opinion that systems theory, as understood by family researchers and practitioners, could be broadened and strengthened by bringing in some of the tenets and contributions of psychosynthesis (McNamara, 1990). This ambitious integration evolved into a fine theoretical dissertation. Another student created an eloquent theory of belonging out of the constructs of self, home, and homelessness (Volkman, 1990).

In summary, positivism maintained that there was a single method, that of the natural sciences, that was valid everywhere. Today postmodern critics are circling like vultures to pick over the spoils of positivism (Smith, 1991). Yet the natural sciences are still very much alive and their commitment to empirical observation and scientific rigor continues to be dominant in social science research. Whereas some critics maintain that the humanities, with their focus on the interpretation of meaning and values, will ultimately serve to provide a superior ideological alternative, that is far from clear. What is clear is the need to begin the research enterprise by asking an essential question and then asking what you must do to convince yourself and others of the validity of the ideas supporting it (Bevan, 1991). Along the journey, be wary of rigid methodological rules and draw on any method with a clear understanding of its advantages, its limitations, and whether it compromises assumptions about the phenomena you are researching.

NOTE

1. An exception is the use of single-subject or $N = 1$ research designs. This is different from the case study approach favored by many qualitative researchers. It is an empirical, quantitative approach associated with specific statistical procedures (cf. Kratochwill, 1978). Single-subject quantitative studies can be used to assess changes in a phenomenon over time through the use of repeated measures or to assess the impact of a particular treatment by removing or "reversing" the intervention and evaluating differences in the dependent variable. Single-subject research strategies are especially appropriate in developing or refining novel interventions and in closely examining the behavior of individual subjects.

PART II

Working With Content: The Dissertation Chapters

Review of the Literature
and Statement of the Problem

The previous chapters provided an orientation to research in the social sciences and offered suggestions on how to develop an appropriate topic. In this chapter the research question begins to take shape, using the vehicle of the review of the literature. A subsequent chapter (Chapter 10) can also be consulted for suggestions on using a personal computer to compile a literature review.

THE INTRODUCTION

The Review of the Literature is generally preceded by a brief introductory chapter. The Introduction consists of an overview of the research problem and some indication of why the problem is worth exploring or what contribution the proposed study is apt to make to theory and/or practice. The Introduction is usually a few pages in length. While it may begin by offering a broad context for the study, it quickly comes to the point with a narrowly focused definition of the problem. The form of the Introduction is the same for both the research proposal and the dissertation itself, although there are likely to be some changes made to the understanding of the research problem after the study has been completed. Ironically, it is usually impossible to write a final Introduction chapter prior to completing the literature review and method, since those chapters will inform the problem and its operationalization.

The wording of the research problem should be sufficiently explicit to orient the most inattentive reader. There is nothing wrong with beginning the chapter with a sentence such as, "In this study I attempted to evaluate the impact of environmental protection legislation on atmospheric pollutants in the chemical industry." The chapter would proceed to stipulate the assumptions and hypotheses of the study, identify the key variables, and explain the procedures used to explore the questions. It should include a synopsis of the arguments that explain the rationale for the research question and the study. It is perfectly acceptable to cite one or more studies that are directly relevant to the proposed investigation and may have inspired it or lent it empirical or theoretical justification. But this is not the place to conduct a literature review. Avoid technical details and keep the Introduction short.

REVIEW OF THE LITERATURE

Often the lengthiest section of the research proposal, the Review of the Literature is placed just after the introductory overview of the study. This chapter of the dissertation provides a context for the proposed study and demonstrates why it is important and timely. Thus this chapter needs to clarify the relationship between the proposed study and previous work conducted on the topic. The reader will need to be convinced that not only is the proposed study distinctive and different from previous research, but that it is worthwhile doing. This is also the place where the student's critical abilities as a scholar are tested and evident. Many students erroneously believe that the purpose of the literature review is to convince the reader that the writer is knowledgeable about the work of others. Based on this misunderstanding, the literature review may read like a laundry list of previous studies, with sentences or paragraphs beginning with the words, "Smith found . . . ," "Jones concluded . . . ," "Anderson stated . . . ," and so on. This is not only poor writing but misses the whole point of an effective review of the literature.

A colleague of ours, Jeremy Shapiro, has noted that much of the labor that goes into writing is often wasted effort because it is not based on a clear understanding of the purpose of an essay or thesis

(Shapiro & Nicholsen, 1986). As a general rule, if you have difficulties in your basic writing skills, that is, in constructing grammatical sentences, using appropriate transitions, and staying focused and concise, a research dissertation will glaringly reveal these weaknesses and the logic and persuasiveness of your arguments will be diminished. One basic suggestion is to obtain remedial help in strengthening basic writing skills. Furthermore, the style of writing that is appropriate to research papers is somewhat different than the style of writing associated with literary prose. Scientific writing tends to be more direct and to the point and less flowery and evocative. Effective writing is an acquired skill that is taken up as a separate topic in Chapter 9.

A good way to formulate a question that is appropriate to a research study is to determine what bothers you (Shapiro & Nicholsen, 1986). As you consider one or more possible questions and draw upon the observations and ideas of others who are interested in the same and related questions, you are in fact formulating the argument. The forum for the argument is the literature review, which is played out in the form of a dialogue between you and the reader. In order to dialogue effectively, the writer must anticipate the kinds of questions and apprehensions that the reader might have in critically examining your argument. It is common for critical evaluations of academic papers to be peppered with comments such as, "What is your point here?" "What makes you think so?" "What is your evidence?" "So what?" The more you can anticipate a reader's questions the easier it will be to formulate your arguments in a way that produces mutual understanding. Dissertations go through many drafts and the revision process consists of asking and responding to these questions from the point of view of a circumspect and knowledgeable reader.

The literature review is not a compilation of facts and feelings, but a coherent argument that leads to the description of a proposed study. There should be no mystery about the direction in which you are going ("Where are you going with this?" is a good question to ask yourself repeatedly in a review of the literature). You always need to state explicitly at the outset the goal of the paper and the structure of the evolving argument. By the end of the literature review, the reader should be able to conclude that, "Yes, of course, this is the exact study that needs to be done at this time to move knowledge in this field a little further along." The review attempts to convince the reader of the legitimacy of your assertions by providing sufficient logical and empirical support along the way. You will continually need to decide what assertions it is reasonable to assume the reader accepts as common understanding and what assertions require data as support. For instance, if you were to assert that survivors of suicide need professional help, a peer reader would probably want to know on what basis you are making that assertion, and request some evidence about the needs of survivors of suicide and why professionals (as opposed to nonprofessionals, for instance) are necessary. On the other hand, the claim that, "Freud was the father of psychoanalysis" is likely to be well established as a fact within the professional psychological community and thus not require further backing.

Becker (1986) reminds us that there is no need to reinvent the wheel and that it is perfectly permissible to draw upon the thoughtful arguments of others and incorporate them into your own research project. This is very much in keeping with our understanding of the incremental, cumulative process that characterizes the development of normal science (Kuhn, 1962).[1] On the other hand, a skillful researcher draws upon original source material rather than relying upon review articles and secondary sources. Becker uses the image of a jigsaw puzzle, in which some of the pieces have been designed by you while others are borrowed in their prefabricated form from the contributions of other scholars. On the other hand, it is worth noting that becoming overly preoccupied with the literature can deform your argument so that you lose your privileged place at the center of the study. In any case, do not neglect to give proper credit to the source of ideas by citing complete references in your writing.

COMMON PROBLEMS

A principal failing of novice researchers at every stage of a project, and especially evident in the review of the literature, is giving away their own power and authority. As a researcher, you need to accept that you are in charge of this study and that, in the case of dissertations, it is likely that you will ultimately be the world's leading expert on the narrow topic you have selected to address. One way of giving away authority is to defer to the authority of others in the review, assuming, for instance, that because Émile Durkheim or John Dewey said something, it is necessarily valid. You need to adopt a critical perspective in reading and relaying the work of others. The main reason why sentences beginning with "Jones found . . ." are best kept to a minimum is that it shifts the focus of the review from your own argument to the work of others. A preferable strategy is to develop a theme and then cite the work of relevant authors to buttress the argument you are making or to provide noteworthy examples of your point or counterexamples that need to be considered. Another way of limiting your own authority is by using quotations in excess. The overuse of quotes tends to deflect the argument away from the control of the author. Restrict the use of quotations to those that are particularly impactful or that are stated in a unique way that is difficult to recapture. Besides, using your own words to present difficult concepts will help convince you (and others) that you really understand the material.

Once you have read the literature in an area, it may be tempting to report everything you now know. Avoid this temptation! A good literature review needs to be selective and it is taken for granted that the majority of source material you have read will not make it directly into the literature review. That does not mean that it wasn't necessary to read all of those books and articles; they provide the expertise required to make your contribution. But remember, in the dissertation itself your task is to build an argument, not a library. One of our colleagues likens the process to a courtroom trial, where all admissible testimony by the witnesses must be relevant to the case and question at hand. Consistently ask yourself, "Why am I including this study or reference?" Similarly, each sentence in the dissertation needs to be there for a purpose, sometimes to provide relevant content and sometimes to facilitate communication to the reader, but never as filler.

The relevant studies need to be critiqued rather than reported. The critique serves to inform the reader about the status of reliable knowledge in the field and to identify errors to avoid in future research. Although the primary task is to build an argument, and you are expected to present your own point of view, it is not fair to exclude references that contradict or question your case. You must be objective enough to present both sides of an argument and acknowledge where the weight of the evidence falls. Throughout the review, leave enough signposts along the way to help orient the reader. One way is to inform the reader of what you have done and what conclusions you have drawn on the basis of the available evidence. You also need to convince the reader that your knowledge of the existing literature is extensive and intensive enough to justify your proposed study.

CRITIQUING A RESEARCH ARTICLE

As you read the available research in an area, you need to maintain a critical perspective, evaluating the study on its own merits and in

comparison to other studies on the same or a similar problem. A
critique does not imply that you must discover and identify a major
flaw or weakness in every study you read. You are evaluating the
content for its application to your research. The following outline
consists of a rather comprehensive set of recommendations for cri-
tiquing a research article. Not all of these items will be included in
any given citation within the literature review. The amount of attention a study receives will depend upon its direct relevance to the
proposed research question and should not detract from the flow of
the argument. Nonetheless, this list can act as a reminder for how to
read and evaluate critically a research article's contribution to a
proposed study:

1. Conceptualization
    a. What is the major problem or issue being investigated?
    b. How clearly are the major concepts defined/explained?
2. Theoretical Framework and Hypotheses
    a. Is there a clearly stated research question?
    b. Are there hypotheses? Are they clearly stated?
    c. Are the relationships among the main variables explicit and
       reasonable?
    d. Are the hypotheses stated in a way that makes them testable
       and the results, no matter what, interpretable?
3. Research Design
    a. What is the type of research design?
    b. Does the research design adequately control for extraneous
       variables?
    c. Could the design be improved? How?
    d. Are the variables clearly and reasonably operationalized? Is the
       choice of categories or cutting points defensible?
    e. Are the reliability and validity of the measures discussed? Is the
       choice of measures appropriate?
    f. Is the population appropriate for the research question being
       studied? Is the sample specified and appropriate? Can the re-
       sults be reasonably generalized on the basis of this sample?
4. Results and Discussion
    a. Are the data appropriate for the study?
    b. Are the statistical techniques appropriate and adequately described?

    c. Are the control variables adequately handled in the data analysis? Are there other control variables that were not considered but should have been?

    d. Are the conclusions of the study consistent with the results of the statistical analyses?

    e. Are alternative conclusions that are consistent with the data discussed and accounted for?

    f. Are the theoretical and practical implications of the results adequately discussed?

    g. Are the limitations of the study noted?

5. Summary

    a. What is your overall assessment of the adequacy of the study for exploring the research problem?

    b. What is your overall assessment of the contribution of the study to this area of research?

LONG SHOTS AND SHORT SHOTS

Our colleague Joseph Handlon has drawn an analogy between doing a literature review and making a movie. In film-making there are "long shots," "medium shots," and "close-ups," which refer to the relative distance between the camera and the subject matter. As a metaphor, a long shot suggests that the material is background for a particular topic. Background material needs to be acknowledged but not treated with the same detail as foreground; it is not figural. A study on the stressful impact of relocation, for instance, might begin with the following observation:

> There have been three basic ways of approaching the topic of stress empirically. One is by regarding stress as an independent variable and focusing on the nature and strength of the stressor, exemplified in the empirical contributions of Holmes and Rahe (1967). A second approach is to view stress as a dependent variable, focusing on the physiological and psychological impact of stressful events, illustrated by the seminal work of Hans Selye (1956). An alternative approach is to view stress as a transaction between a stimulus and a response, which is moderated by a set of cognitive variables. This approach, elaborated in the work of Lazarus and his colleagues (Lazarus & Folkman, 1984), forms the conceptual foundation for this study.

In this way, considerable literature can be referenced without attending to details or critical evaluations of each study.

The medium shot is somewhere between the long and the short focus and requires a bit more descriptive material. As an example, let us assume that a researcher wishes to explore the effect of social protest and threats of violence on the well-being of workers in abortion clinics. It would be appropriate to obtain a good overview of the impact of potentially violent social protest in other contexts, as well as a good understanding of the emotional demands of working in a clinic serving women with unwanted pregnancies. Studies that bear on these relevant issues may not need to be presented in critical detail, but certainly need to be summarized sufficiently to give the reader a clear indication of the status of the research as it pertains to the orientation of the proposed study.

Finally, the close-up requires a careful examination of the research and is reserved for those studies that have the most direct relevance to the proposed research question. In some cases, this might refer to one or two studies that are being modified or amended in some critical way to form the basis for the current study. More frequently, it refers to a collection of work on a relatively narrow topic that is clearly central to the proposal. These studies are not merely referenced but critically examined, so that the reader obtains a clear sense of what is already known about the phenomenon, how reliable and valid the conclusions based on that work are apt to be, and how the proposed study will deal with previous limitations and move the field ahead. The researcher who is interested in exploring the impact of infertility treatments on communication between husbands and wives might present the following close-up statement after having carefully described the samples, measures, and procedures of the two most relevant (fictitious) studies in that literature.

> Of the two studies that bear directly on the proposed question, Sterile (1986) found that couples reported improved communication after experiencing prolonged infertility treatment, while Ripe and Fertile (1987) concluded that behavioral exchanges between infertile couples more frequently escalated into arguments the longer that medical interventions continued. Of particular concern in Sterile's study is the fact that because men and women were interviewed together, the couples may not have been totally honest and their responses may have been prejudiced by one another. Beyond this threat to validity, the conflicting findings of the two studies suggests the need for a more

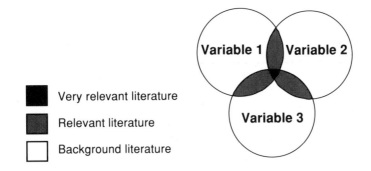

Very relevant literature

Relevant literature

Background literature

Figure 4.1. Venn Diagram Guide to the Literature Review

definitive investigation of the impact of infertility treatment on communication patterns within couples.

A good strategy for reviewing the literature can be found by referring to a Venn diagram (see Figure 4.1) of three intersecting circles, which is derived from the previously discussed exercise on formulating research questions. The long shots, or wide angle lenses, are represented by the portions of the three primary variables that are independent of the other two variables. The medium shot is illustrated by the intersections of any two variables. The close-up, or narrow-angle lens, refers to the joint intersection of all three variables. As a general rule, any studies in the existing literature that incorporate all of the major variables or constructs that are present in the proposed study will require very careful scrutiny because they are particularly relevant. Studies that relate some of the variables (e.g., two) also deserve a short description. Studies that deal with only one of the selected variables, perhaps in conjunction with other, less relevant variables, are merely background. They are generally too numerous to examine in detail and include a great deal of content that does not pertain to the current study. Certainly, one need not review all studies dealing with sexual dysfunctions, for instance, in order to focus on male impotence in mid-life. Nor will one need to consider all previous work on men or mid-life. Yet gender issues and mid-life development issues may provide important background material and a theoretical foundation for the proposed study. Moreover, the researcher will not have to introduce every study on impotence but will probably need to be familiar with a broad range of previous work in the area.

STATEMENT OF THE PROBLEM

At the conclusion of the literature review, the reader should have obtained a fairly clear idea of the study. By this time you will have carefully crafted your argument and moved the reader along as you build your case. You will have convinced your reader of your mastery of the subject matter by having reviewed and critiqued the existent literature that pertains to your study and gives it a suitable context. The next immediate challenge is to form a transition between the literature review and the next section of the dissertation, the Statement of the Problem. One way to build this transition, so that the literature review chapter appears connected to the proposed study, is to write a summary of the review you have conducted. This summary would highlight your main conclusions, including reference to the most relevant literature (which you have previously reviewed), and leave the reader anticipating the next steps.

The Statement of the Problem is sometimes written as a separate chapter and sometimes located at the very end of the Review of the Literature. Although you have probably offered a general statement of the problem early in the introductory chapter of the dissertation, this is the place for a more specific statement. The specificity of the problem statement is very important. A research problem consists of much more (and less) than a misunderstood collection of unidentified relationships. The statement is usually framed in the form of one or more research questions and research hypotheses. Although we recommend the inclusion of formal hypotheses as a general standard, whether or not to include them may depend on the type of study, what is known about the question, and the conventions of your discipline and department. Similarly, the statement of the problem may contain conceptual definitions of major concepts. This is particularly true when competing definitions of the concepts exist within the field of inquiry (e.g., it might be important to point out that the study will focus on trait anxiety as opposed to state anxiety or other conceptualizations of the construct of anxiety).

It is critical that a research question have an explanatory basis. This means that the statement of the problem contains a brief summary of the conceptual underpinnings for the proposed research. *Dust bowl empiricism* is the derogatory term used to refer to a shotgun approach to research, in which the investigator levels his or her sights to see what is out there without developing a convincing chain of presuppositions and arguments that lead to a prediction. There is no research problem in "wondering" how the variables of gender, voice quality, and persuasion intercorrelate, so this will not pass for a suitable problem statement. Hypotheses have the virtue of being explanatory expressions of research questions because they imply a commitment to a particular understanding of how variables relate.

An example of a research question without a specific hypothesis is, "What is the role of male significant others on the criminal activities of female criminals?" This research question implies a study that obtains information from or about women who have been convicted of crimes regarding the influence of boyfriends and male acquaintances in their criminal activities. A study that poses this question without predictive hypotheses (perhaps because of a lack of available information about this topic) might be termed "exploratory."

In most instances it is possible to project hypotheses, even in those instances where there is a relative lack of research in an area. This is because there are apt to be studies and theories on related topics that can inform the proposed study. In the above example, the investigator may have developed some reasonable hunches about the research question from her knowledge of women's developmental theory and the role of the peer group in criminal behavior. These hunches would be reflected in one or more hypotheses. An example of a research hypothesis is: "There is a negative relationship between positive body image and motivation for augmentation mammoplasty." A second example is: "Couples in stable, unhappy marriages use more conflict avoidance methods than couples in stable, happy marriages." The first hypothesis suggests a study in which the variables of body image and motivation for breast augmentation will be statistically correlated, while the second hypothesis suggests a study using two groups of couples who will be compared on how they manage conflict. In either case, the variables specified in the hypotheses will need to be *operationalized,* that is, clarified with regard to how they are to be measured. Such specification usually takes place in the Method chapter. In the first example, the researcher might predict, as did one of our students, a negative relationship between scores on the Jourard-Secord Body Cathexis Scale and a 10-item Likert-type scale of motivation to seek augmentation mammoplasty (Ewing, 1992). It is obviously important to specify each and every variable. In the second example, the terms *stable/unstable marriage,* and *conflict avoidance methods* would need to be articulated, and the two groups of couples would need to be identified.

It usually takes several rewritings in order to come up with research questions and hypotheses that are optimally clear, concise, and meaningful. Note that hypotheses are typically written in the present tense and they are written as positive assertions. They are not written as "null" hypotheses. The reader may be aware that inferential statistics work on the assumption of rejecting null hypotheses, that is, hypotheses that assume there are no significant differences between or among groups or no significant relationships among variables. Research hypotheses, on the other hand, should not be stated as null hypotheses, but as directional hypotheses (or hypotheses that specify a relationship between variables) that follow from the argument that has been established in the preceding chapter. As research hypotheses, null hypotheses are only confusing, since they reflect the opposite of the argument you have been proposing. If the logic behind the stated hypotheses is not totally evident, it is always a good idea to follow or precede each hypothesis with a short rationale that reminds the reader how it emerged out of theoretical propositions established in the review of the literature.

One recommended statement of the criteria for a good hypothesis is that it (a) be free of ambiguity, (b) express the relationship between two or more variables, and (c) imply an empirical test (Locke, Spirduso, & Silverman, 1987). A common pitfall is to have more than one hypothesis embedded in a single, complex statement (e.g., "Women who earn more than their husbands have more self-confidence, more friends, and receive more help on household tasks than women who earn less than their husbands").

Some dissertations contain both research questions with hypotheses and research questions that stand alone. The hypotheses might cover those relationships that directly challenge previous work or test a theory, while research questions without hypotheses are more open-ended opportunities to satisfy your curiosity. For instance, a student studying self-disclosure patterns among psychotherapists might have specific hypotheses about the relationship between self-disclosure and friendship (e.g., "Therapists who are high in self-disclosure with their patients have fewer personal friends") but no clear expectations about the relationship between self-disclosure and stages of therapy (e.g., "What is the relationship between therapist self-disclosure with patients and the stage of psychotherapy?").

Another way of combining research questions and hypotheses is to use research questions as more general investigatory themes, which are then followed by specific hypotheses that make predictions in a testable form. This example is very loosely based on a recent dissertation by one of our students (Davenport, 1991):

Research question: How do dyslexic adolescents cope with the effects of their learning disabilities?

Hypothesis #1: Dyslexic adolescents who accept the diagnosis of having a learning disability use more problem-focused coping strategies than dyslexic individuals who reject or deny the diagnosis.

Hypothesis #2: Dyslexic adolescents who accept the diagnosis of having a learning disability rely more on social support than dyslexic adolescents who reject or deny the diagnosis.

Hypothesis #3: Dyslexic adolescents who reject or deny the diagnosis of having a learning disability use more avoidant coping strategies than dyslexic adolescents who accept the diagnosis.

Hypothesis #4: Dyslexic adolescents who reject or deny the diagnosis of having a learning disability deny negative affect more than dyslexic adolescents who accept the diagnosis.

The statement of the research problem, together with the precise exposition of the research questions and/or hypotheses, serves as a transition between the review of the literature and the description of the methods of the study. The following chapter offers guidelines and suggestions for presenting the methods.

NOTE

1. Kuhn has also identified "paradigm shifts" as discontinuous, more disruptive changes in the evolution of scientific thinking.

Box 4.1

STUDENT SUGGESTIONS

1. Use the APA style manual at the outset. It is much easier to get into the habit of referencing articles and books correctly than to go back and revise the format at a later time. This is especially true for direct quotes, where it is critical to keep page numbers! A software program such as Manuscript Manager will make it much easier to use APA format conventions automatically within the text and for references.

2. You'll know when to stop your literature review when the articles you read become redundant and when the authors and articles that are cited become familiar to you.

3. Develop a system for organizing and cataloging what you read. I began to note, in the margins of the books and articles I read, numbers representing the topic being covered. I just started numbering as I discovered topics and I ended up with 38 topics that included everything I wanted to be able to retrieve. Later on I organized the references according to the numbers in a computerized filing program.

4. Read the original writings of the theorists you are studying, not just what someone else says about their theories. I have found that other people tend to misinterpret original writings. Piaget, for instance, is terribly misunderstood in America. Plus, the original source is so much richer. Trust yourself before you trust others. Take your time to pinpoint those parts that aren't completely clear to you, since those are usually higher level thoughts that you need to struggle to understand.

5. One of the problems that students will likely encounter is tracking a given subject matter through different disciplines, for example, social psychology, sociology, anthropology, communications, cross-cultural studies, and so on. Often research in one discipline is isolated from another not by differences in philosophical orientation but rather by the sociological barriers of a fragmented academia. The subject matter may even have a different name for the same basic phenomenon. Scanning basic textbooks in these different fields can give you clues to follow-up in the library directory. Journals are extremely valuable in following academic debates between members of a research tradition or identifying battles between research traditions. Bibliographies can be very useful in tracking down new sources.

Box 4.1, continued

6. It is much easier to record complete references for source materials when you initially read them than later on. It is very frustrating and time-consuming to retrieve a publication date or page number after an entire paper has been written!

7. Use an ample number of subheadings in your Review chapter in order to maintain organization and flow. Make sure that your headings convey enough information to assist and orient the reader to the material that follows.

5 ✔

The Method Chapter: Describing Your Research Plan

The Method chapter of a dissertation, article, or proposal describes the exact steps that will be undertaken to address your hypotheses and/or research questions. For this reason the Method section follows logically from the statement of the problem in much the same way as research questions follow from the review of the literature. The goal of this chapter is to provide a clear and complete description of the specific steps to be followed. It is necessary to describe these steps in sufficient detail to permit a naive reader to replicate your study.

In Chapter 3 we suggested that students select a suitable problem before selecting the appropriate method with which to study that problem. However, in some dissertations the "method" may in fact be the topic of study. A student may become excited about the possibilities of a particular data collection technique or method prior to generating a suitable problem. In most cases, however, the appropriate method of study is generated by careful consideration of the research questions and the applicable method by which those questions may be studied. The following material is divided into two major sections, one that focuses primarily on the quantitative dissertation and one on the qualitative dissertation; we strongly recommend, however, that the student read both sections. The issues to be considered are not independent of one another and there is considerable overlap in the content of this chapter regardless of the method being employed.

THE METHOD CHAPTER
IN A QUANTITATIVE DISSERTATION

The Method chapter is the place in which the exact steps you will be following to test your question(s) are enumerated. The Method chapter typically contains the following three subsections; Subjects or Participants, Instrumentation or Measures, and Procedures. In addition, the Method chapter of a dissertation proposal often contains a "Statistical Analysis" or "Data Analysis" section in which procedures for approaching the data are outlined. Research that utilizes special equipment frequently contains an "Apparatus" section in which the nature and type of equipment used is described.

A frequent mistake contained in first drafts of Method chapters involves the overuse of the chapter as an opportunity to rehash the material contained in the review of the literature or statement of the problem chapters. This chapter should primarily be viewed as a set of directions for conducting a specific piece of research. We follow this perspective in describing each of the subsections of a Method chapter below.

HOW TO BEGIN A METHOD CHAPTER

A reasonable way to begin a Method chapter is to develop an introductory paragraph that describes both the design of the study and organization of the chapter. This prepares the reader for what is to follow and provides a framework within which to incorporate the materials. This paragraph says to the reader, "This is the Method chapter, this is how it is organized, and this is the type of design I used." The most difficult component of the introductory paragraph may appear to be the design statement. There are dozens of books that take "research design" as their sole topic. Our purpose here is not to review this extensive material. In this context we are suggesting only a short sentence or two that informs the reader of the general type of design and any suitable label that may be applied to it.

For example, imagine a study in which you plan to mail 700 surveys to retired male executives in an attempt to assess their adjustment to retirement. It is probably sufficient to simply state something like the following: "This study utilized a cross-sectional survey design to assess adjustment to retirement of a sample of retired male executives." Similarly, imagine an experimental design in which two dichotomous variables will be used as independent variables. It may be sufficient to describe the design as "an experimental study utilizing a 2 × 2 factorial design." An example of such a design is described in a dissertation by Sangster (1991):

> An experimental, 2 × 2 factorial, pretest-posttest design was used to test the hypothesis. The independent variables were (a) training type and (b) management experience. Respective levels of independent variables were descriptive and prescriptive training, and high and low management experience.

Determining exactly what type of design description best fits your study can be accomplished by reference to one of the many texts that describe designs (e.g., Campbell & Stanley, 1966; Kerlinger, 1977), but a specific label may not be as important as a clear explanation of the structure of your study. For example, a study by Macdonald (1990) examined the relationships among empathy, personal maturity, and emotional articulation. She described her design as follows,

> The research design was a correlational design utilizing cross-sectional survey methodology and includes a number of survey instruments. The purpose of the design was to correlate the scores of the personality tests listed below with the scores on responses to the short stories, as well as measure the interrelationship of the responses to the short stories.

DESCRIBING YOUR SAMPLE

The Subjects section of the Method chapter describes the source and number of subjects you will be using (in a proposal) or the source and number of subjects actually obtained (in a completed project). Note that we use the term *subjects* in a very broad context. The subjects may be informants or participants in the research, organizations or events, documents or segments of commercials edited from television programs, or even an entire society, as in the case of anthropological research. In studies of human beings, the term "participants" may be preferable to the term "subjects." The concern in this section of the Method chapter is to describe why and how the particular unit of analysis was selected.

A frequent problem we have observed is that students often confound a description of the sampling of subjects with the procedures used to collect data from these subjects. The former belongs in the Subjects section while the latter belongs in the Procedures section. Of particular importance in the Subjects section are the specific sampling procedures used, the rationale for selecting a given number of subjects, and the source of the subjects. What type of sample will you draw: random, stratified, purposive? Where will your subjects be located? How many subjects are necessary for your particular design? Each of these questions is important and should be dealt with in the Subjects section. We discuss each in turn below.

The Sampling Design. As is the case with research design in general, the issue of sampling is a complex one. Our purpose, however, and your purpose as researcher, is not to discuss the knotty problems of sampling. Your job is to describe how you will accomplish this task in your study, taking all of the theoretical and practical issues into account. A knowledge of the various types of sampling design is a prerequisite to developing an appropriate description of your particular sampling problem. Two examples may be of assistance in developing your approach. In a recent dissertation examining gender differences in professional identity among practicing psychotherapists, New (1989) obtained a mailing list of all licensed psychologists in the state of California. Beginning at a randomly selected start point she then sampled every Nth name until she had exhausted the list. Her dissertation describes this process as follows:

> A systematic random sample was drawn from a list of all psychologists who have been licensed in the state of California for five or more years. The sample was obtained from a research center specializing in the distribution of selected sampling lists. A table of random numbers was used to locate the initial sampling point. Every 20th person was selected such that an initial group of 400 was obtained. These persons were mailed the study materials.

In a second instance, illustrating a nonrandom procedure, Caddell (1989) selected students from classes at three universities to examine moral education in the college environment. He describes his sampling procedure as follows:

64 WORKING WITH CONTENT

The questionnaire was administered to selected undergraduate and graduate level classes at California State University-Fullerton, California Baptist College and Pacific Christian College. The sample was divided into a subset from the morally nondirective institution (Cal State-Fullerton, $N = 178$) and a subset from morally directive institutions (Cal Baptist College, $N = 104$ and Pacific Christian College, $N = 71$).

Locating Subjects. Of the two examples presented above only one describes both *where* and *how* the subjects were obtained as well as the sampling design used. In the study using university students, Caddell (1989) fails to describe how the "selected undergraduate and graduate level classes" were obtained. In fact, the procedure was one of asking professors at each institution for permission. This decidedly nonrandom procedure could probably best be described as a "convenience" sample.

The Appropriate Number of Subjects. The appropriate number of subjects for a given design is one of the most difficult sampling problems. Generally, given considerations of cost and time, students wish to obtain as few as their committee will allow; however, this decision is not arbitrary. Most students tend to underestimate the number of subjects necessary to draw meaningful conclusions from the data. For example, imagine a study from the field of education in which the researcher wishes to compare the level of creativity of students who are sent to public schools as compared to those who receive home schooling. If in fact there is a difference, the student-researcher must collect enough data for this difference to appear in the results. The smaller the difference is, the more data must be collected to find it.

The best method to approximate the number of subjects is to conduct a *power analysis*. A power analysis lets the researcher know how many subjects are necessary in order to detect any effects due to the independent variables, given (a) the size of the effect of these variables, (b) the type of statistical tests to be utilized, and (c) the level of significance (or alpha level) of the study. The level of power, expressed as a probability, lets the researcher know how likely he or she is to avoid a Type II error. A Type II error occurs when one fails to reject the null hypothesis even though it is false. Failing to reject a false null hypothesis means that an effect existed, but was not detected by the study. As the probability of a Type II error increases, the power of the study decreases. In fact, power is equal to one minus the probability of a Type II error. Thus, if a probability of a Type II error is .15, power is .85 $(1 - .15 = .85)$. Power calculations may be difficult to conduct and students and their committees frequently rely on general rules of thumb to determine the appropriate number of subjects. Computer programs now simplify these calculations and we strongly recommend that they be used in dissertation planning.

In the example of the student interested in comparing the home schooled with the traditionally schooled youngster, a t test might be used to compare levels of creativity between these two groups. The table below gives an example of a power analysis designed to answer the question: "How many subjects will I need to test the difference between the means of two groups, if I use a level of significance of .05 and desire a power of .80?" Table 5.1 shows the number of subjects necessary to obtain the specified power level of .80 (a standard level, generally considered acceptable) using an alpha level of .05 (also a generally acceptable criterion) if the size of the effects (i.e., the mean differences) are small, medium or large.

Table 5.1 Power Analysis for a t test

To achieve a power level of .8, while setting the level of significance (alpha) at .05.		
Effect Size	N Per Group	Total N
Small	393	786
Medium	64	128
Large	26	52

Table 5.1 shows that if medium effects were predicted, it would require 64 subjects per group to achieve a power of .8 when using an alpha level of .05. Even if the effects are large, it would require at least 26 subjects per group to achieve the same power level (.8). Another way to say this is that, even if the research hypothesis is true, the researcher may fail to support this hypothesis with an insufficient sample size. As the sample size increases, it becomes more likely that the statistical tests will detect any effects that exist in the data.

Finally, it is important to make two critical points about the use of power analysis. First, in many dissertations the use of power analysis may be unrealistic. This may be due to the fact that enough subjects to meet the requirements of a purely mathematical procedure may not exist. Similarly, qualitative dissertations, case studies, oral histories, and intensive interviews may rely more on what the student and committee deem reasonable to develop a convincing argument, independent of statistical testing. Second, in cases where quantitative analysis is essential, students often use a multivariate framework with many variables. The number of subjects necessary in these contexts is likely to be many more than that suggested above for a simple two-group t test.

INSTRUMENTATION:
DESCRIBING YOUR RESEARCH TOOLS

The Instrumentation section of a Method chapter describes the particular measures you will employ and how they will measure the variables specified in your research questions and hypotheses. This section "makes your case" for the use of particular measures as the best and most appropriate to your specific research environment.

If you are using instruments that have been used previously, particularly standardized and widely recognized scales, then you should consider the following three areas as particularly relevant to your description: (a) information about the appropriateness of the use of the instrument with the population and setting described in the proposal, (b) information about the measurement characteristics of the instrument, and (c) information about the administration and scoring of the scales. Each of these three areas will be discussed separately below.

Is the Measure Appropriate? A number of scales may exist that measure the same phenomenon. How is the researcher to select which is the "best"? (Or how does one guard against the claim that he or she should have used something else?)

The first step is to support the use of a given instrument with the population selected for your study. Measures that work well with adults may not be particularly effective with adolescents or children. Measures designed for use in one culture may work very poorly in another. The writer's goal is to locate empirical studies that demonstrate the utility of an instrument with a population as closely representative of the population to be used in his or her study as possible.

The second step is to demonstrate that the authors of the measure you select conceive of the phenomenon in terms similar to the manner in which you have conceptualized the same phenomenon. For example, all measures that assess depression are not the same because those who originally designed the measures have viewed depression from different theoretical positions. The content of the measures reflect these different positions. Thus it may be important to indicate that you have chosen a particular instrument because it reflects the conceptualization of the phenomenon in a manner that is consistent with your position.

What Are the Measurement Characteristics of the Instrument? By measurement characteristics we mean the reliability, validity, and structure of the measure. *Reliability* refers to the ability of a measure to produce consistent results. *Validity* indicates that a measure in fact measures what it purports to measure. *Structure* refers to the number and meaning of subscales contained in a given instrument. For example, the Bell Object Relations Reality Testing Inventory (Bell, 1988) contains 90 items, 45 of which assess object relations and 45 of which assess reality testing. Within each of these broad divisions there are additional subscales, four for object relations and three for reality testing. This breakdown describes the structure of the measure. A complete description of the measurement characteristics of this instrument would also contain information about the reliability and validity of the total scale, scores for object relations and reality testing, and information about the seven subscales.

It is important to realize that in a *proposal* the only information likely to be available regarding an instrument's reliability and validity is that which is contained in the existing literature. After the student has collected his or her data it is important to add to this body of literature by reporting on the reliability and validity of the instrument as evidenced in the new sample. The reliability of an instrument is a characteristic of the population in which that instrument is used. Thus an instrument that achieves high reliability in one sample, will not necessarily receive that same level of reliability in another sample representing a different population.

How Does One Administer and Score the Measures? It is important for the reader to understand how an instrument is administered and scored. Some measures are self-administered and may simply be mailed or passed out with instructions to "check the box that most represents your feelings at the present time." Others, such as the Rorschach, require extensive training to administer and score. For others, the scoring methods are a well-guarded secret and completed protocols must be sent to a central location for computerized scoring (for a fee, of course). Sometimes it may be sufficient to include a copy of the instrument, with instructions to the respondent, in an appendix; however, this is usually not appropriate with copyrighted instruments.

The example below provides what we consider to be a clearly written description of a rather complex instrument. It is drawn from a recent doctoral dissertation (Hardwick, 1990). The section we quote contains information about the structure, scoring, and administration of the instrument. Information about the reliability and validity of the instrument is contained in materials we have not chosen to quote here:

> The Bell Object Relations Reality Testing Inventory (BORRTI) is a 90-item "true-false" self-report inventory which was used to operationalize the dependent variables, object relations and reality testing. The BORRTI was administered to each participant (see Appendix K). It yields four object relations (OR) subscales and three reality testing (RT) subscales. Each dimension, OR and RT, is measured by 45 items which are worded to reflect various levels of object relations and reality testing. The four OR subscales are: Alienation, Insecure Attachment, Egocentricity, and Social Incompetence. The three RT subscales are: Reality Distortion, Uncertainty of Perception, Hallucinations and Delusions. The test also yields a quasi-summary score for each overall OR and RT construct. This score is the sum of all items to which the participant responded in a pathological direction. Thus, a participant could conceivably have normal subscale scores while still responding to any number of pathological OR and/or RT items.

The author then goes on to describe examples of test items and the meaning of each subscale, including the interpretation of high and low scores, and the measurement characteristics of each subscale, including the reliability and validity demonstrated in recent research.

THE USE OF COPYRIGHTED SCALES

Copyrighted scales are not reproduced in a dissertation or research publication. In order to use copyrighted scales in a study, permission should be obtained in writing from the holder of the copyright.

WHAT IF I DESIGN MY OWN INSTRUMENTS?

In rare instances a student may not be able to locate any existing measures that tap the construct he or she desires to measure. Our first recommendation is to send the student back to the library with the instruction "keep looking." This advice reflects our strong belief that developing your own instrument is generally not a good idea. Research based on hastily thrown together instruments, which lack sufficient pretesting and are questionable in terms of reliability and validity, is of little scientific value. If the student is unable to locate a satisfactory instrument, he or she may wish to consider changing the focus of the research from one that attempts to relate the construct in question to other constructs, to one that attempts to design and assess a new instrument, a valid dissertation topic in and of itself. In this case, building the instrument becomes the central topic, and examining its relationships to other variables becomes part of the process of establishing the validity of the new instrument.

It is not uncommon for a student to modify questions or add additional questions to validated instruments to facilitate the purposes for which the instrument is to be used. For example, when using some instruments with younger populations it may be necessary to reword or eliminate questions regarding relations with the opposite sex. Questions such as, "My sex life is satisfactory" may not be appropriate for seven-year-old children.

Our position is that the modification of an existing instrument is perfectly acceptable, but that such changes may make the norms invalid and may affect both the reliability and validity of the instrument. A close examination of many instruments currently in use reveals that there has been considerable borrowing among various authors over a lengthy time period. When borrowing and/or modification occurs it becomes the responsibility of the student to justify such changes and make his or her case for the reliability and validity of the instrument in its revised form.

It is often advisable to use an existing instrument in conjunction with a new instrument of the student's design. Even if the student feels that his or her instrument is "better," the use of multiple measures of a single concept can be very useful when establishing the reliability and validity of a new instrument. Of course, when a new instrument fails, as they often do, the old standard can be used in its place.

Most dissertations contain some form of "demographic data sheet." These contain questions that assess gender, ethnicity, years of employment, marital status, education, and the like. While such questions need to be carefully thought through, we do not consider adding such questions to a battery of existing instruments in the same context as "scale development." We suggest examining surveys from the National Opinion Research Center general social survey (National Opinion Research Center, 1990) for examples of how to solicit "demographic information."

Research that concentrates on instrument development is a valuable enterprise and often makes greater contributions than research that attempts to relate existing measures to each other in some new and as yet untried fashion. Nevertheless, such research requires large numbers of subjects, frequent retesting, and sophisticated statistical models. Both the student and his or her committee must carefully weigh the pros and cons of undertaking such an enterprise.

WHAT IF I AM NOT USING A QUESTIONNAIRE TO COLLECT DATA?

Questionnaires are not the only type of data collection instrument. Behavioral observations, extended interviews, and archival data all constitute valid sources of data for dissertation research. The sources of this information, as well as checks for reliability and validity of the information, will need to be considered. For example, a recent dissertation (Newton, 1990) examined the incidence of depression, substance abuse, and eating disorders in the families of anorexics. Data were obtained from existing medical records. Newton supports his data collection procedures as follows:

> A number of authors have studied the validity of data found in medical records (Harlow & Linet, 1989; Horwitz, 1986; Paganini-Hill & Ross, 1982; and Hewson & Bennett, 1987). Horwitz (1986) compared epidemiological data collected from medical records and by interview for 462 subjects who were part of a case-control study of chronic disease. Results showed that agreements between medical record and interview data are variable, and depend on the type of data examined and the strategy for handling incomplete or ambiguous responses. Horwitz did find a 93% (0.02 Kappa) agreement between medical records and interviews for family history of breast cancer. (p. 45)

In the above quote the author lets the readers know that (a) he is aware of potential problems with his method, (b) he has read the literature, and (c) the literature supports the validity of this technique in some instances.

Special considerations are also involved with designing interviews. The ability to construct questions that elicit open and honest responses is a skill that must be learned, as is the ability to conduct such interviews. The student should refer to one of the many excellent references such as Douglas (1985) or Mishler (1986) for advice on developing and administering the extended interview.

PROCEDURES: DESCRIBING HOW
YOU DID (OR WILL DO) IT

The Procedures section provides a detailed description of the exact steps taken to contact your research participants, obtain their cooperation, and administer your instruments. After reading this section one should know when, where, and how the data were collected. For example, in a mailed survey, one might describe the following steps: (a) mail precontact letter, (b) one week later mail survey packet, (c) two weeks later mail follow-up survey for nonrespondents. Exact copies of the precontact letter and cover letters accompanying the survey measures should be provided in appendices. Note that the sampling procedures have been described in the Subjects section and the measures described in the Instrumentation section. There is no need to repeat this information in the Procedures section. When procedures are complex and require the administration of multiple instruments over multiple time periods a flow chart or table presenting the procedures visually becomes very helpful.

It is important that any information that might potentially affect the number of participants or their characteristics be included in this section. For example, much social research is conducted with college students. Were the students asked to volunteer? Were they given extra credit? Was participation mandatory as part of a course requirement? Similarly, when administering mailed surveys such simple information as whether the addresses were handwritten or mailing labels were used can affect response rates. Such information is critical to replicating the experiment and understanding the exact nature of the population sampled. It is also important to describe the procedures undertaken to gain access to the population. For example, if working with high school students, was it necessary to obtain permission of the school board or the principal, or did one simply sample all of their sixth-grade classes? Finally, the procedures for obtaining informed consent should be described in detail and a copy of the informed consent statement, if any, provided in an appendix. This is particularly important when working with minors, who are legally not permitted to provide their own consent to participate in research. (Chapter 12 contains a more detailed discussion of informed consent and other ethical issues.)

Typically, instructions to subjects, as well as ethical release forms, are included in the Appendices. The ethical release forms are crucial because they inform subjects about the potential hazards of participating in the study (e.g., emotional upset), limits to confidentiality, and use of the data, and make it clear that participation is voluntary. (In some rare instances participation may not be voluntary.) The purpose of the release forms is protection both for you and for those who participate in your research. Release forms also force you to think about the implications of your study on the physical and emotional well-being of humans or animals employed as subjects. Most universities have stringent procedures for conducting ethical research, which generally include passing proposals through a Human Subjects Committee. A sample copy of a typical human subjects release form can be found in Chapter 12. These forms should include a description of the study, the right of refusal, an explanation of risks and potential discomfort, an opportunity to withdraw without penalty, and the potential for feedback.

DATA ANALYSIS: HOW TO JUSTIFY AND DESCRIBE AN ANALYSIS

A research proposal often includes a statement that describes the statistical tests that will be used to address the hypotheses and research questions. This section is usually the one that scares students the most (because students learn statistics in the abstract, not as applied to specific research questions). The great benefit of including this statement is that it forces you to think through how you will treat the data from your dissertation at the time the proposal is generated, rather than after the data are collected. Time spent thinking about these issues at the proposal stage saves considerable time and pain later. In this way one can avoid spending countless hours collecting data that are ultimately not analyzable because they are not in the correct format in the first place. In the next chapter we describe in detail how to present the results of a study once the data have been analyzed. In this section we discuss how to "propose" a particular sort of analysis prior to having actually undertaken it.

There are a number of reasons why this section is particularly difficult, beyond the fact that students may not be prepared to apply statistics to their own research. First, statistical analysis is virtually never a one-shot affair. Data may be analyzed and reanalyzed many times before the researchers are satisfied that the data have been given the correct treatment. A technique that initially seemed perfectly reasonable will later seem inappropriate due to the number of cases or distributions presented by the completed sample. Second, interesting questions often arise after initial analyses are completed. If a hypothesis is not supported, one may search for control variables that might help explain the lack of support. For example, a hypothesis may be supported only among the highly educated. Research with a large number of noncollege graduates in the sample may obscure the relationship until the college graduates are analyzed separately from the noncollege graduates.

What, then, is the student to do? First, we strongly recommend that, in consultation with your advisors, and experts if necessary, you describe which technique seems most appropriate given: (a) the nature of your hypothesis, (b) the number of independent and dependent variables, and (c) the level of measurement of each of the variables. The following chapters contain recommendations regarding the use of statistical techniques. There are also computer programs that assist with the selection of statistical techniques and statistics texts which present flow charts directing students to appropriate statistical methods. Figure 6.1, in the following chapter, reproduces one such chart from the work of Tabachnik and Fidell.

Do not turn your data analysis section into a treatise on a particular technique paraphrased from a statistics text. Rather, present a short, reasoned statement that a particular technique seems most appropriate. An example of a straightforward data analysis proposal is provided by Connell's (1992) study of stress in psychotherapists.

> The primary hypothesis, that there will be a significant difference between Group 1 and Group 2 on level of stress, will be tested using a one-tailed t test. . . . The expectation that Group 2 will score differently than Group 1 in 12 of the subscales of the Essi System StressMap will be tested using a multivariate analysis of variance (MANOVA).

SHOULD YOU DISCUSS THE LIMITATIONS OF YOUR RESEARCH?

A final section of the Method chapter that we encourage students to include in a dissertation proposal is a statement on "Limitations and Delimitations" of the study. Delimitations imply limitations on the research design that you have deliberately imposed. These delimitations usually restrict the populations to which the results of the study can be generalized. For example, you may decide to study only males, either because the theory upon which your hypotheses are based has not been studied in females, or because you have a readily accessible population of males, but not females. Limitations, on the other hand, refer to restrictions in the study over which you have no control. For example, you may be limited to only a narrow segment of the total population you wish to study, or you may be limited by the method you elect to use.

THE METHOD CHAPTER IN A QUALITATIVE DISSERTATION

Qualitative studies must meet the same criteria for completeness that quantitative studies do, that is, they must be able to describe in sufficient detail the methods and procedures to permit replication of the study. It may not be possible to predict some components of the procedures in a qualitative study with the same degree of precision as in a quantitative study. This does not mean, however, that qualitative studies are not planned or that this planning must not be well described.

Research questions based on what has been called phenomenological psychology (Giorgi, 1985; Keen, 1975), naturalistic inquiry (Lincoln & Guba, 1985), or qualitative research (Marshall & Rossman, 1989) require methods based on a different philosophical orientation than that utilized by rationalistic inquiry. Phenomenological research adopts views of sampling, instrumentation, and data analysis that are often directly contrary to the views held by those conducting more traditional "rationalistic" inquiry. Lincoln and Guba (1985) call this "The Paradox of Designing A Naturalistic Inquiry" and argue that, "The design specifications of the conventional paradigm form a procrustean bed of such a nature as to make it impossible for the naturalist to lie in it—not only uncomfortably, *but at all*" (Lincoln & Guba, 1985, p. 225). Nevertheless, Lincoln and Guba outline a broad series of design considerations that, in some respects, go beyond those required by conventional methodologies. These considerations describe what must be considered, in advance, in order to prepare a naturalistic study. These 10 design considerations are reproduced below.

1. Determining a focus for the inquiry
2. Determining fit of paradigm to focus
3. Determining the "fit" of the inquiry paradigm to the substantive theory selected to guide the inquiry
4. Determining where and from whom data will be collected

  5. Determining successive phases of the inquiry
  6. Determining instrumentation
  7. Planning data collection and recording modes
  8. Planning data analysis procedures
  9. Planning the logistics
 10. Planning for trustworthiness

The above 10 "elements of a naturalistic design" cover what we would identify as the Statement of the Problem and Method chapters of a proposal. The first three (focus, fit of paradigm to focus, and fit of paradigm to theory) pay explicit attention to the assumptions that underlie a study, and the fit of these assumptions to the methods being used. Thus Lincoln and Guba (1985) seek to make distinct the fit between the purpose of the study, the basic guiding principles underlying the approach, and the substantive theoretical framework. Often this "fit" is assumed in much research when in fact it should not be. The lack of fit between purpose, approach, and theory in research may become apparent when findings and conclusions seem to make no apparent sense in light of the original questions.

The fourth element mentioned above, determining where and from whom data will be collected, is directly analogous to our consideration of "sampling." However, the naturalistic approach to sampling is quite different from that of the rationalist. According to Lincoln and Guba:

> The naturalist is likely to eschew random or representative sampling in favor of purposive or theoretical sampling because he or she thereby increases the scope of range of data exposed (random or representative sampling is likely to suppress more deviant cases) as well as the likelihood that the full array of multiple realities will be uncovered. (p. 40)

As described by Bailey (1992),

> phenomenological research uses sampling which is idiographic, focusing on the individual or case study in order to understand the full complexity of the individual's experience. From this perspective, there is no attempt to claim an ability to generalize to a specific population, but instead, the findings are relevant from the perspective of the user of the findings. (p. 30)

The sixth element above, determining instrumentation, is analogous to the Instrumentation section of a proposal described earlier;

however, the instrument of choice for the naturalist is the human observer. Thus naturalists place particular emphasis on improving the human observer and make no claims for the "reliability and validity" of the instrument in the rationalistic sense. The task for the student proposing an observational study would be to place considerable emphasis on the training and practice of the observer(s).

Naturalistic researchers also recognize the utility of other more traditional sorts of instrumentation, provided that these are grounded in the central focus of the research and axioms underlying the method. Typically our students have used interviews to generate discussion surrounding the major research questions. For example, Barth (1987) designed an interview schedule to examine female mid-life transitions and Shallenberger (1986) designed a schedule to examine the "coming out" process of gay males. In both instances the task of the instrumentation section was to (a) describe the interview, and (b) demonstrate how the interview served as a sufficient device to focus discussion on the research questions of the study. Questions of reliability and validity are posed differently in this setting because these interviews serve to focus discussion between the researcher and research participant, producing data that are textual rather than numerical. (See Chapter 3 for further discussion of the naturalist's interpretation of reliability and validity.)

Issues of determining the successive phases of a study (#5), planning data collection and recording modes (#7), and planning the logistics (#9) are subsumed under what we have described as Procedures. Regardless of the sort of study one is conducting, attention must always be paid to how the data are to be collected, independent of the form that the data might take. Data recording may be described along two dimensions, fidelity and structure. A recorded interview, for example, has high fidelity and little structure, while a standardized paper and pencil test has both high fidelity and high structure. We recommend the use of tape recorders to record interviews and place little reliance on the use of field notes. However, the use of a diary or journal to record impressions, reactions, and other significant events that may occur during the data collection phase of research can be a useful source of information and we encourage this practice.

Naturalistic studies may involve multiple interviews, a return to the field after a period of time, or "member checks" with participants to reconsider the interpretations of the data made by researchers. Thus Lincoln and Guba (1985) make specific reference to the "phases" of a research project and the importance of "logistical considerations."

Often the analysis of the data in one phase will be conducted before the next phase begins. We recommend that, when a study involves multiple time points, a table be presented that describes each time point and the operations to be carried out within that time point. Lincoln and Guba group the logistical considerations into five categories, as follows: prior logistical considerations for the project as a whole, the logistics of field excursions prior to going into the field, the logistics of field excursions while in the field, the logistics of activities following on field excursions, and the logistics of closure and termination.

The issue of data analysis (#9) is probably more problematic for those considering naturalistic inquiry than it is for those undertaking conventional quantitative research. As Lincoln and Guba (1985) state, "Not very much can be said about data analysis in advance of the study." This leaves the student in a difficult position, particularly if a committee is clamoring for a Data Analysis section.

The fact of the matter seems to be that quite a bit can be said about data analysis within the context of naturalistic studies. Chapter 12 of Lincoln and Guba's *Naturalistic Inquiry* (1985) considers the issue of "processing naturalistically obtained data" in considerable detail. Marshall and Rossman (1989) describe five steps in the analysis of qualitative data, and Miles and Huberman (1984) devote an entire text to the issue of qualitative data analysis. We consider some of these works in more detail in the following chapter. The main point is that, even though a student may not be able to refer to specific statistical procedures, we believe the general framework of an analysis may be specified in advance. Students should expect that both qualitative and quantitative dissertations are likely to involve multiple phases of data analysis.

The issue of trustworthiness (#10) is a general term representing what conventional researchers think of as internal and external validity, reliability and validity, and objectivity. Naturalistic researchers have developed their own language to describe these terms, laid out in an outstanding article by Guba in 1981, and described in Chapter 3. In order to complete a proposal utilizing naturalistic methods the student must master the language of the naturalistic paradigm of inquiry. This permits the student to utilize terms such as *member check* and *audit trail* meaningfully, in much the same way as students using conventional methods take courses to learn the meaning and importance of terms such as *internal consistency reliability*. In naturalistic research the "trustworthiness" of the design becomes the standard upon which it is likely to be judged, and the

Box 5.1

STUDENT SUGGESTIONS

1. Pilot test any instruments you use, whether you make them up yourself or they are standard research tools. Every person can misread or misunderstand something different. It also helps to ask your pilot subjects specific questions, such as inquiring if a section was interesting or difficult.

2. I was amazed how well-known instruments can contain vague or ambiguous items. You can't trust that other researchers have constructed scales that will be appropriate for your use. If you want to compare your results to scores reported in the literature, however, you can't tamper with the instrument.

3. If you decide to construct your own instrument, never start with demographic items. Most researchers put them at the end. They are boring. Be sure your questionnaire looks nice and aesthetic. Questionnaires done on dot matrix printers go in the trash. It must be clear and easy to understand. Put your response alternatives in columns rather than rows. It is easier for the eye to follow.

4. It helps a lot to give an incentive to subjects. Include a stamped, self-addressed envelope. Most important is personal contact. My committee thought I would get a 10% return rate from a mailing to APA members, so I made sure to contact people who had access to subjects directly.

5. One relatively inexpensive way to encourage subjects to participate is to offer a lottery or drawing for money, a gift certificate, or some item of value. That way it will not cost an arm and a leg to pay every subject but create a really worthwhile reward for one or a few subjects.

Method section becomes a major component upon which this judgment is based.

This concludes the presentation of the basic elements of a Method chapter for a thesis or dissertation. When the study is completed and the Results and Discussion chapters have been added to the document, it will be necessary to go back to the Method chapter and change the verb tense from future to past. We also recommend removing the section on data analysis from the Method chapter and incorporating that material into the Results chapter.

Presenting the
Results of Empirical Studies

The purpose of a Results section is to present the findings as clearly as possible. In order to do this it is necessary to plan the presentation before one writes it. The major difficulty students have is that they do not begin with a plan about the order in which to present material and tend to place too much material in the Results section. In most dissertations the Results section contains JUST THE FACTS: tables, figures, transcript summaries, and the author's description of what is important and noteworthy about these. Extended discussion of the results, though very important, belongs in the Discussion section. Additional literature summaries, a rehash of the conceptual framework or methods, are unnecessary and detract from the purpose of the Results section. The counterexamples to these general organizing principles may be observed in social science disciplines such as political science, sociology, and education. Some departments may encourage students to present the results and discussion as a single, interrelated chapter. We are aware of this alternative format, and agree that in some cases it may improve the readability and flow of the dissertation. Nevertheless, we base the organization of this chapter on the assumption that the student's dissertation will contain separate Results and Discussion chapters.

How should the results be organized? There is no one standard answer that applies to every case, and it may not matter, IF: (a) there

is an organizational logic that can be described to the readers, and
(b) one does a good job of leading the reader through the results.
However, a few suggestions might be of benefit. First, the results
should be organized in such a way that the reader is not confronted
with a large mass of data. The task is to give a simple, clear, and
complete account of the results, without getting into an extended
discussion of the meaning of the findings, and without rehashing all
the information in all the tables. LEAD THE READER CAREFULLY
THROUGH THE FINDINGS, MAKING SURE THAT THE READER
KNOWS WHAT YOU CONSIDER TO BE THE IMPORTANT OB-
SERVATIONS.

WHERE TO BEGIN?

Most Results sections begin with a description of the sample.
Simple demographics (sex, marital status, age, etc.) can be presented
in written or tabular form. If the unit of analysis is not a person, then
variables that describe the characteristics of the unit being studied
should be presented. For example, if the unit of analysis was the city,
then it might be appropriate to describe the population, population
density, ethnic composition, median house price, and so on. This
gives the reader a picture of the basic unit or units comprising the
study. Such information may be presented in a table, a figure, or
simply discussed in the text. It depends on what gives the reader the
best overall picture of the results. It is not necessary to provide the
reader with raw data, but one must make sense of the data for the
reader. (If you are not sure which way to present the data, try
presenting it in different ways and ask a friend to read the different
presentations, and always consult with your committee.)

ADDRESSING RESEARCH QUESTIONS
AND HYPOTHESES

After describing the sample, the next step will probably be to
address research questions and/or hypotheses. Sometimes it may be
appropriate to address one at a time under separate subheadings,
but subheadings such as "Hypothesis 1" tend not to work. This is

because more than one hypothesis is often addressed by a single analysis, and use of a hypothesis number as a section heading provides little information. It seems much more effective to create subheadings that describe the content of the hypothesis being addressed. For example, "The relationship between anxiety and employee performance," seems to make a better heading than "Hypothesis two." It also may be awkward to use subheadings that isolate a single statistical procedure, such as "Results of Analysis of Variance." This is because a number of statistical procedures may be needed to address a single question, such as the relationship between performance and anxiety suggested above. One method that appears to work is to address one research question at a time. This may involve the discussion of the results of several different statistical analyses and the test of several different hypotheses. But every situation is different, so remember the main goal, a clear and simple presentation.

For example, suppose you are interested in susceptibility to group influence. One *research question* (there would probably be more than one) might ask about the specific relationship between gender and conformity. (Conformity is one indicator of group influence.) One *research hypothesis* (there may be more than one) might be that females are more conforming than males. The specific *statistical hypotheses* might be that: (a) mean conformity rates for females will be equal to or less than the mean conformity rate for males (the null hypothesis) and (b) mean conformity rate for females will be higher than that of males (the alternative hypothesis, suggesting a specific direction of influence to be examined by a one-tailed statistical test). In the above design a one-tailed t test would probably be used. If the null hypothesis was REJECTED, the alternative hypothesis would be supported, thus providing support for the research hypothesis.

It would probably be best to organize the results around answering the *research question(s)*. The above question concerning the relationship between gender and conformity would compose one section, comprising a separate subheading. One or more paragraphs of this subheading would present the analyses. Each analysis would specifically address one or more *statistical hypotheses*. When all of the analyses relating to this research question have been presented and explained, the analyses relating to the next *research question* would be presented.

One should try to avoid presenting tremendous amounts of data, but this is not always possible. Complex studies, with many measures, may leave the author no choice but to present a large amount of information. The more data that must be presented, the greater the burden on both the author and the consumer. Later in this chapter some hints for reducing large amounts of data are presented. Sometimes it is appropriate to note that certain findings were not significant, without actually presenting the findings, but this is usually NOT appropriate if the findings confront major hypotheses. Accept the fact that, as an author, you are in a better position to judge the importance of specific findings than anyone else, and organize the results to emphasize what is important. It is reasonable to ignore or give passing reference to what is unimportant, but remember that there is a difference between what is unimportant and what fails to support your hypotheses. The material that follows is directed primarily to quantitative analysis and we devote only a small amount of space to the issue of qualitative analysis at the end of this chapter. We suggest that the reader read both sections.

THE NUTS AND BOLTS OF DESCRIBING QUANTITATIVE RESULTS

The Results section usually presents the outcome of multiple analyses of data. Each analysis can be broken down into a series of different statements. These statements present the major findings, some of which may also be presented in tabular or graphic form (i.e., in tables and figures). The major focus, however, remains the text, and the presentation of important findings, together with test statistics, within the text. An explanation of four different types of statement is given below.[1]

Statement Type I. Refers the reader to a table or a figure and describes what is being measured or presented.

   Example 1—Describing a table of correlations.
      The correlations between student ratings and final examination marks are given in Table 1.
   Example 2—Describing a table of percentages.
      Table 1 presents the percentage of responses for each of the five possible categories.
   Example 3—Describing a table of means.
      Table 1 presents the means and standard deviations by drug category.

Statement Type II. Describes the major findings shown in a table or figure. Comparisons of means, standard deviations, frequencies and r values between the various conditions represent examples. Frequently these sentences are combined with the third type of statements discussed below.

Example 1—Description of correlational table or figure.
Of the 10 correlations, it can be seen that 9 are positive and 8 are above $r = .32$.
Example 2—Description of an experiment.
Males rated applicants as lower in intelligence and friendliness when wearing cologne. In contrast females rated the applicants higher in intelligence and friendliness when wearing cologne.
Example 3—Description of figure.
As shown in Figure 2, the rate of typing increased from a baseline of about 0.7 words per minute to about 1.5 words per minute during the treatment period.

Statement Type III. Presents the results of a statistical (inferential) test, such as F or t. These statements are typically combined with statement type II.

Example 1—Describing correlations.
Six of the correlations between amount of homework and GPA were found to be positive and significant ($p < .05$).
Example 2—Describing an experiment.
The retention of communication content was found to vary significantly as a function of the time and method of measurement, $F (2, 80) = 34.45$, $p < .01$.
Example 3—The image instructed groups were significantly faster ($F (1, 60) = 7.34$, $p < .01$) and made fewer errors ($F (1, 60) = 9.94$, $p < .01$) than the no image groups.

Combining Statement Types II and III.

Example 1—Describing correlations.
The correlation between mean parent IQ and child IQ was statistically significant, $r (190) = .87$, $p < .05$.
Example 2—Describing an experiment.
The mean score for females (75.5) was significantly greater than the mean score for males (70.7), $F (1, 28) = 23.1$, $p < .05$.

Statement Type IV. Summary statements of the major findings or conclusions.

> Example 1—The results suggest that students who reported very heavy drug use had significantly higher maladjustment scores than other students.

The statements above provide examples of the variety of comments that might be used to describe the results of an empirical study. When describing results try to avoid editorializing with such statements as, "Unfortunately, the findings were not significant . . ." or "This result was quite surprising . . ." Such statements do little to enhance the reader's understanding of the results and may make your writing appear sophomoric.

PRESENTING TABLES AND GRAPHS

GENERAL CONSIDERATIONS

Nearly all dissertations contain one or more tables or figures (i.e., graphs) designed to organize the results of statistical analyses. This section, and the sections that follow, presents the basic principles and logic of describing statistical analyses. The first question an author should probably ask him or herself is, "Should these results be presented in a table, a figure, or simply described in writing?" Generally, a table containing only a few numbers is unnecessary. For example, a table showing the sex distribution in a sample is unnecessary. This information could be adequately covered in the text by simply stating the percentage of males or females in the sample. However, in a study with many groups, where the sex distribution within each group is important, it would probably be more efficient to present this information in tabular form.

Similarly, many dissertations contain graphic presentations of data. These are usually called "Figures." A figure may be a chart, graph, photograph, line drawing, or just about anything else that is not a table. The decision to use a figure is an important one and should be thought through carefully. Figures take considerable space and may clutter a dissertation rather than make it easier to follow. For example, there is little value in using bar charts to present information that can be easily and economically displayed in a table, unless the presentation dramatically illustrates a comparison that is not readily apparent from a table. Students may become enthusiastic about their ability to produce bar and pie charts with existing computer programs; however, the tendency to fill a dissertation with such charts should be avoided.

A great deal of thought needs to precede the construction of tables and figures. Not only does their number and content need to be thought through, but the specific organization of each needs to be planned so as to best illustrate the important aspects of the analysis. In addition, you may be required to meet the formatting demands of your university or style requirements of an organization such as the American Psychological Association (APA). In this chapter we follow the guidelines of the American Psychological Association for constructing tables, and in Chapter 12 we discuss how to describe results in text in accordance with APA guidelines. It should be pointed out that the APA requirements are somewhat dated in that they require table titles to be underlined. Underlined titles are changed to italics in APA journals, but dissertation table titles remain underlined in final versions of dissertations. In order to be consistent with these conventions we have underlined the table titles in this chapter only. You should check both your department's and your library's requirements before assuming that the exact format presented here is adequate for your needs.

A few simple procedures can greatly improve the look and readability of tables regardless of the specific requirements of your university. First, even though computer analyses produce values with many decimal places, a rounded value often conveys information more clearly than a value with many decimal places. Is there really any logic to reporting that 36.92273% of the sample was single, when you can simply report that 37% were single? (It is generally only important to report correlations or covariances to three decimal places to facilitate the reproduction of analyses based on these values. Otherwise, keep it simple.) Second, values can be compared down columns more easily than across rows. The following two sections suggest that percentages in univariate (one-variable) and bivariate (two-variable) tables be calculated within columns. Third, column and row averages and totals can provide much additional information, without cluttering the table. Finally, it is unnecessary, and undesirable, to cram every number on a computer printout into a table. Select the information to be included carefully, organize it to make the information visually appealing, and use plenty of white space to improve visual organization.

The tables and figures in a Results section should relate to one another and to the text. This relationship should be represented in both the structure of the tables and use of language. Tables and figures should use similar formats and results should be organized similarly. If a table refers to a measure or scale using a particular designation, the same designation should be used in all tables, figures, and the text. The author's familiarity with the scales and measures used in a dissertation will not be shared by most readers. If something is referred to as an "inventory," it should be referred to as an inventory throughout, not as a scale, battery, or subscale. If one refers to "reaction time" in the text, this should not become "response latency" in a table.

THE PARTS OF A TABLE

Tables typically contain five major parts: number, title, headings, body, and notes. Each of these is briefly described below. More detailed discussion directed toward specific types of tables, such as frequency distributions, crosstabulations, and analysis of variance are presented in the following sections.

Numbering Tables

Every table must be numbered. The American Psychological Association suggests that all tables be numbered with Arabic numerals in the order in which they are first mentioned in the text. Begin with Table 1, and continue throughout. Do not use Table A, Table B, and so forth, and do not use Roman numerals (Table I, Table II, etc.). Do not number tables within chapters (Table 3.1, Table 3.2, etc.) and do not number tables containing related or similar information with letters (Table 5a, Table 5b, etc.). Consider instead combining the tables. The only exception to these rules concerns the numbering of tables within appendices. The third table in appendix B is Table B-3. The first table in appendix A is Table A-1.

Table Titles

Every table must have a title. Generally a good title presents the name of the major variable or variables and type of analysis, but does not contain information that unnecessarily lengthens the title. Information that can be presented in headings of the table does not have to be in the title. Good table titles often take considerable trial and error to construct. The following sections, which highlight specific types of analysis, give many examples of clear table titles, as well as completed tables to use as guidelines. The American Psychological Association suggests that all table titles be underlined and that major words be capitalized.

Table Headings

Headings tell the reader what variables are being presented and establish the organization of the table. It is considered legitimate to use abbreviations for headings, including "f" for frequency, and "%" for percent, but the meaning of the abbreviation should be obvious. DO NOT use computer mnemonics or variable names, and do not use scale acronyms without including a note as to their meaning. For example, a mnemonic used with the National Opinion Research Center general social survey is XMARSEX. Most people would not realize that this refers to the respondent's attitude regarding extramarital sex and it is not advisable to use such mnemonics as labels in tables. Similarly, many persons might assume that BDI refers to the Beck Depression Inventory, but a note to this effect must be included in a table that uses BDI as a heading.

Table Body

The table body contains the numbers, or data. As indicated above, do not clutter the table with unnecessary numbers, and round numbers to improve readability. Numbers that can be calculated quickly on sight (i.e., a table with two columns of small numbers, such as five and seven) could probably do without a "total" column. When cells of the table are empty, it is customary to enter a dash (—) to indicate that no data are contained within the cell. This prevents the reader from thinking that a number was inadvertently left out.

Table Notes

There are three kinds of table notes: general notes, specific notes, and notes indicating the statistical significance of findings, called probability notes. A general note is indicated by the word "Note." APA format requires that this be underlined and followed by a period. General notes are used to provide information referring to the table as a whole, including the meaning of symbols or abbreviations. For example, one would use a general note to indicate that BDI referred to the Beck Depression Inventory. Specific notes are used to refer to the content of a specific cell and are given superscript lowercase letters, beginning with the letter "a." Specific notes should begin in the upper left of a table and be lettered from left to right across table rows. Probability notes indicate the outcome of significance tests. Asterisks are used to indicate the probability levels, one asterisk being used for the lowest level, two for next lowest, and so on. Probability notes usually appear at the bottom of tables as follows:

$^*p < .05.\ ^{**}p < .01.\ ^{***}p < .001.$

A one-tailed test may be distinguished from a two-tailed test by using an alternative symbol in the probability notes. For example:

$^*p < .05$, two tailed. $^{†}p < .05$, one tailed.

There are two very important points to remember about notes: First, notes are relevant to only one table. Thus, just because you used a note to define BDI in one table, it is not appropriate to assume that it need not be defined in future tables. Second, probability notes need not be consistent across all tables. Thus, one asterisk may indicate $p < .05$ in one table and $p < .001$ in the next.

Finally, thinking regarding the use of probability notes is changing. While the most recent version of the APA manual still suggests the use of probability notes, some have pointed out that this procedure was developed during a period when it was necessary to use tables showing critical values for different levels of significance (.05, .01, .001). Computer programs currently print the exact probability of a given outcome, making the use of such tables outdated. The information contained in these probabilities may be important in understanding the meaning of results. For example, a probability value of .049 might be reported a $p < .05$, but a value of .051 might be reported as not significant, despite the very small difference between these two numbers. Even if the latter finding is considered too large to reject the null hypothesis, the information contained in these numbers may be of value in interpreting the results. Thus it seems reasonable to inquire of your committee regarding the use of probability notes as opposed to the presentation of exact probability values in your Results section.

PREPARING THE DATA FOR ANALYSIS

The first type of "results" information likely to be presented in a dissertation is a description of the sample. The researcher is likely to present a number of one variable (or univariate) tables called *frequency distributions*. Some standard guidelines for the presentation of frequency distributions will be discussed below. The first consideration, however, is to guarantee that the data have been tabulated correctly. Whether working by hand or with a computer, correct tabulation of the results is a necessity. The following steps outline the process leading to the production of both meaningful tables and reasonable statistical analysis.

STEP 1: IS THE VARIABLE IN THE CORRECT FORM?

Mutually Exclusive Categories: The variable must be constructed so that each observation may be placed in one and only one category. For example, demographic descriptions often include a "Marital Status" item that includes the categories single, married, divorced, widowed. It is possible that a person could check both the single and divorced categories. This pattern may be reduced or eliminated by wording the question to read, "Are you currently never married, divorced," and so on.

When questions assume the "Check all that apply" character, each response must become a separate variable. For example, when assessing a respondent's feelings, behavior, and experience related to a parent's alcohol use, a checklist of items is presented and instructions are to "Check all that occurred in your family." Responses include, "Lost sleep because of a parent drinking," "Ever heard parents fight when one was drunk," and "Wish parent would stop drinking." Items in the checklist each become a separate variable, with a "Yes" and "No" code. The sum of the "Yes" codes becomes a new variable that can be used to assess the extent of the damage from alcoholism within the family.

Exhaustive Categories: Every item in a questionnaire, scale, or instrument must have a response for every case, even if the response is "Not Applicable." Thus frequency distributions and their tables must include the percentage of "Valid Responses," those for which meaningful answers were obtained, and the number of invalid responses, often called "Missing Values," for which irrelevant or meaningless answers occurred. When working with frequency distributions check to make sure that you can account for (i.e., exhaust) the entire sample for every distribution. (This prevents having to figure out after the fact where some of your data went.)

Missing Values: Observations that do not fit logically into a variable's meaningful categories must also be accounted for in order to produce a set of exhaustive categories. Those that do not fit into these "meaningful" categories are called missing values. Missing values may occur in a variety of ways.

1. No response, no answer
2. Uncodable responses
3. Incorrect measurements or broken equipment
4. Lost data, subjects that cannot be located

Most computer programs permit special codes, called missing value codes, to allow the program to separate the meaningful responses from the missing values. The number of missing values is usually reported in a table note. When the number of missing values is added to the number of valid responses the entire sample should be accounted for.

STEP 2: GROUPING THE DATA

The second step is to place the data for each observation (i.e., each case or subject) into one of the variable's categories. Though this is often done with a computer, the example in Table 6.1 below illustrates how this might be done by hand. The data are from a study of campus suicide by R. H. Seiden (1966). Seiden used records of campus police to classify the methods of suicide used by college students at U.C. Berkeley.

Table 6.1 Example Table

Method	Tally	Frequency
Firearms	11111 111	8
Poison	11111 1	6
Asphyxiation	1111	4
Hanging	11	2
Jumping	11	2
Cutting	1	1
		23

Computer printouts of frequency distributions look quite different than this but contain the same basic information. Some examples will be presented at the end of this section.

STEP 3: CREATING A CORRECTLY LABELED TABLE

Creating a frequency distribution does not complete the process of making the distribution presentable and easily understood. The table that you create must be correctly labeled and identified. In addition, you may need to satisfy the requirements of the library or publication that will receive the information. Some general rules, consistent with APA guidelines, are presented below.

SOME GUIDELINES FOR CREATING CORRECTLY CONSTRUCTED AND LABELED TABLES

THE CONTENTS OF A COMPLETE TABLE:

1. A table number
2. A table name or title that includes the name of the variable and some information about the sample or population
3. The set of mutually exclusive and exhaustive categories you have developed (The headings)
4. Frequencies, percentages, and totals (The body)
5. Notes, including the source, if the data are not original

DEALING WITH MISSING VALUES

Sometimes missing data may create a problem when constructing tables. These problems may be dealt with in a number of ways:

1. Create a category to contain the missing data
2. Footnote the number of missing values
3. Create a residual category for all unimportant values

ARE THERE GUIDELINES FOR SPACING IN TABLES?

The APA guidelines require that every line in a table be double spaced. However, we have never seen a dissertation that follows this requirement to the letter. This is because the requirement is primarily for journal articles being submitted for publication. We recommend that our students use spacing to make the tables readable and we follow that guideline in the materials presented in this chapter.

An example of a correctly labeled table using the data from the suicide study is provided in Table 6.2.

EXAMPLES: CONSTRUCTING ONE VARIABLE (UNIVARIATE) TABLES AND STATEMENTS THAT DESCRIBE THEM FROM COMPUTER PRINTOUTS

The two examples that follow are both taken from the 1988 National Opinion Research Center General Society Survey. The GSS draws data

Table 6.2 Methods of Suicide Used by Students at UC Berkeley (1951-1962)

Method	f	%
Firearms	8	35
Poison	6	26
Asphyxiation	4	17
Hanging	2	9
Jumping	2	9
Cutting	1	4
	23	100%

Note. From "Campus Tragedy: A Study of Student Suicide," R. H. Seiden, 1966, Journal of Abnormal and Social Psychology, 71.

from a national sample of all noninstitutionalized adults in the United States, 18 years of age or older. The data were processed using the personal computer version of the Statistical Package for the Social Sciences (SPSS-PC+). Two variables are considered. The first assesses how frequently the respondent attends religious services. This variable was given the name ATTEND by those who developed the survey. The second variable, given the name PARTYID, assesses political party preference. The computer printout is presented in Table 6.3, and the correctly labeled table with frequencies and percentages in Table 6.4. Short summary statements concerning the tables are also presented.

Table 6.3 Sample Computer Printout Showing the Frequency of Attendance at Religious Services

ATTEND		HOW OFTEN R ATTENDS RELIGIOUS SERVICES			
Value Label	Value	Frequency	Percent	Valid Percent	Cum Percent
NEVER	0	254	17.2	17.2	17.2
LT ONCE A YEAR	1	108	7.3	7.3	24.5
ONCE A YEAR	2	168	11.3	11.4	35.9
SEVRL TIMES A YR	3	194	13.1	13.1	49.0
ONCE A MONTH	4	116	7.8	7.8	56.8
2-3X A MONTH	5	143	9.7	9.7	66.5
NRLY EVERY WEEK	6	109	7.4	7.4	73.9
EVERY WEEK	7	277	18.7	18.7	92.6
MORE THN ONCE WK	8	109	7.4	7.4	100.0
DK, NA	9	3	.2	MISSING	
	TOTAL	1,481	100.0	100.0	
Valid Cases 1478	Missing Cases 3				

Table 6.4 Frequency of Attendance at Religious Services

	f	%
Never	254	17.2
Less Than Once a Year	108	7.3
Once a Year	168	11.3
Several Times a Year	194	13.1
Once a Month	116	7.8
2-3 Times a Month	143	9.7
Nearly Every Week	109	7.4
Every Week	277	18.7
More Than Once a Week	109	7.4
Don't Know, No Answer	3	0.2
Total	1,481	100.0

Note. From National Opinion Research Center General Social Survey, 1988.

The following statement might be used to describe Table 6.4.

Table 6.4 presents the distribution of attendance at religious services. Approximately 19% of the sample state that they attend church every week, while about 17% never attend.

Table 6.5 presents the computer printout and Table 6.6 the correctly labeled table derived from it, with frequencies, percentages, and cumulative percentages.

Table 6.5 Sample Computer Printout Showing the Frequency Distribution of Political Party Preference

PARTYID		POLITICAL PARTY AFFILIATION			
				Valid	Cum
Value Label	Value	Frequency	Percent	Percent	Percent
STRONG DEMOCRAT	0	233	15.7	15.8	15.8
NOT STR DEMOCRAT	1	313	21.1	21.2	36.9
IND, NEAR DEM	2	180	12.2	12.2	49.1
INDEPENDENT	3	186	12.6	12.6	61.7
IND, NEAR REP	4	140	9.5	9.5	71.2
NOT STR REPUBLICAN	5	275	18.6	18.6	89.8
STRONG REPUBLICAN	6	146	9.9	9.9	99.7
OTHER PARTY	7	5	.3	.3	100.0
		3	.2	MISSING	
	TOTAL	1481	100.0	100.0	
Valid Cases 1478	Missing Cases 3				

Table 6.6 Political Party Affiliation of a Random Sample of U.S. Residents

Party Affiliation	f	%	Cum %
Strong Democrat	233	15.8	15.8
Not Strong Democrat	313	21.2	36.9
Independent Near Democrat	180	12.2	49.1
Independent	186	12.6	61.7
Independent Near Republican	140	9.5	71.2
Not Strong Republican	275	18.6	89.8
Strong Republican	146	9.9	99.7
Other Party	5	0.3	100.0
Total	1,478[a]	100.0	100.0

Note. From National Opinion Research Center, General Social Survey, 1988.
a. Three cases did not provide valid answers.

The following statement might be used to describe Table 6.6.

Table 6.6 presents the percentage distribution of political party preference. Almost half of the respondents stated that they thought of themselves as Democrats, or Independents near Democrats (49.1%). Another 38.3% thought of themselves as Republicans or Independents near Republicans.

Note the treatment of missing values in the tables under discussion. In Table 6.3 the Frequency column shows 3 missing values. The Percentage column indicates that this is .2% of the sample, while the Valid Percentage column computes the percentage after excluding these 3 missing cases. These two columns are almost identical because three cases are a small percentage of the total. In Table 6.4, constructed from the printout shown in Table 6.3, all 1,481 cases have been presented, including the 3 receiving the "Don't Know, No Answer" code (i.e., the missing values). In Table 6.6, constructed from the printout shown in Table 6.5, the frequency column excludes the 3 missing cases, and the total (1,478) is given a note to indicate that the 3 cases have been excluded. The percentage column in this table is constructed from the Valid Percentage column in Table 6.5.

HOW TO CONSTRUCT AND INTERPRET TWO-VARIABLE (BIVARIATE) TABLES

BIVARIATE DISTRIBUTIONS

Bivariate distributions, usually presented in the form of tables, are the basic ingredients of many dissertations in the social sciences, education, and business. It is therefore important to understand clearly the information these tables contain and how to construct the tables in such a way as to extract information correctly. This section concentrates on the general principles involved in constructing bivariate tables and interpreting bivariate relationships by using percentages.

THE GENERAL FORM OF A BIVARIATE TABLE

A bivariate table (also called a cross-tabulation or contingency table) contains the joint distribution of two variables. The categories of each variable are laid out in the form of a square or rectangle containing rows (representing the categories of one variable) and columns (representing the categories of the other variable). The general form of a bivariate table containing two variables is presented below for two variables X and Y.

$$
\begin{array}{ccc}
 & X & \\
 & x_1 \quad\quad x_2 & \\
 \quad y_3 & & \\
Y \quad y_2 & & \\
 \quad y_1 & &
\end{array}
$$

In the above example the letter X represents the variable whose categories form the columns and the letter Y refers to the variable whose categories represent rows. Thus if X represents the response to a question indicating whether or not the respondent has ever had children, and Y represents attitudes toward abortion, our table might appear as follows:

	EVER HAD CHILDREN	
	YES	*NO*
ATTITUDES AW		
TOWARD AAW		
ABORTION NW		

AW = Always Wrong
AAW = Almost Always Wrong
NW = Never Wrong

CELL ENTRIES AND MARGINAL TOTALS

The entries that occur in each cell will be the frequencies representing the number of times that each *pair* of values (one from each variable) occurs in the sample. These are called *cell frequencies.*

The entries that occur at the end of each row or column are called *marginal frequencies* and represent the total number of times the category of the row variable or column variable occurred.

By adding either the row marginal frequencies or the column marginal frequencies you obtain the total N (total sample size).

HOW TO DECIDE WHICH IS THE ROW VARIABLE AND WHICH IS THE COLUMN VARIABLE

The conventional way to construct a table is with the independent variable at the top and the dependent variable at the side of the table. Thus, as in our example above, the letter X is used to identify the independent variable and the letter Y the dependent variable.

An independent variable is presumed to cause or determine a dependent variable. If we discover that attitudes toward abortion are partly a function of parenthood (i.e., parents are more opposed to abortion than nonparents) then parenthood is the independent variable and attitudes toward abortion is the dependent variable.

A dependent variable is the variable that is assumed to depend on or be caused by the independent variable. If you find that income is partly a function of amount of education, income is being treated as a dependent variable.

SUMMARIZING THE INFORMATION IN A BIVARIATE TABLE

Table 6.7 includes frequencies for the Attitudes Toward Abortion by Parenthood table described above.

What we want to do is examine Table 6.6 in such a way as to summarize the information meaningfully and to explore the hypothesis that parenthood influences attitudes toward abortion. Notice, however, that we have a different number of parent (YES) and nonparent (NO) respondents. Thus, we cannot compare the YES with the NO distributions (across the different columns) unless we standardize these distributions. The most frequently used standardizing measure is the percentage, but what is the most sensible way to percentage this table?

Table 6.7 Bivariate Table Showing the Relationship Between Attitudes Toward
          Abortion and Parenthood

		EVER HAD CHILDREN	
		YES	NO
ATTITUDES	AW	269	320
TOWARD	AAW	175	153
ABORTION	NW	52	93

AW = Always Wrong
AAW = Almost Always Wrong
NW = Never Wrong

To calculate percentages, we may work within columns, within rows, or with the total sample of 1,170 observation (i.e., Total *N*). Thus Table 6.6 may be percentaged in three different ways. Depending on how a table is constructed, only one of these ways may provide meaningful answers to the question of the relationship between the two variables. Given our recommendation to place the independent variable as the column variable, the appropriate method of percentaging is within the columns (i.e., up and down each column).

When working within columns the column marginal total becomes the base number used for the total. For example, to find the percentage of Always Wrong (AW) answers among those with children we take the number of AW responses in that column and divide it by the total number in that column and then multiply the total by 100 (269 / 496 × 100 = 54%).

Some texts and dissertation manuals may recommend placing the independent variable in the rows of the table. If this is the case remember to calculate percentages within the rows (i.e., across each row).

THE CONCEPT OF ASSOCIATION BASED ON
SUBGROUP COMPARISONS

The final step is to compare the conditional distributions with each other after the percentages are computed within each column. This allows us to compare the percentage responding Always Wrong, Almost Always Wrong, and Never Wrong across the YES and NO, or Parent and Nonparent categories.

In doing this, notice that we have a definite routine in mind. We calculate percentages in one direction and make our comparisons in

Table 6.8 Correctly Percentaged Bivariate Table Showing the Relationship
Between Attitudes Toward Abortion and Parenthood

		Ever Had Children	
Attitudes Toward Abortion	*Yes*	*No*	*Total*
Always Wrong	54%	47%	50%
	269	320	589
Almost Always Wrong	35%	30%	32%
	175	201	376
Never Wrong	11%	23%	18%
	52	153	205
Total	100%	100%	100%
	496	674	1,170

another direction. Because we compute percentages up and down
the columns, we compare across the columns.

To examine the hypothesis that parenthood influences attitudes toward abortion we can use a few simple rules. If each conditional
distribution is identical to each other conditional distribution, then we
say that the two variables involved are independent of each other or are
not related to each other. If the conditional distributions are different,
then the two variables are said to be related. To make this more clear,
examine Table 6.8, which has been percentaged appropriately.

A SIMPLE STATISTIC: THE PERCENTAGE
DIFFERENCE

One easy method of making a statement about the degree or
amount of relationship in a table is to compare the percentages in the
conditional distributions. This measure is called a *percentage difference,* and is most appropriate for small tables like the one discussed
above. As an example of how this measure might be calculated and
used, compare the 54% of the parents who believe that abortion is
always wrong with the 47% of nonparents who believe that abortion
is always wrong. The difference is 7%. You can now state that 7%
more parents than nonparents believe that abortion is always wrong.
A similar comparison can be made between the parents and nonparents with regard to the belief that abortion is never wrong. The
percentage difference in this comparison is 12%.

Table 6.9 Means and Standard Deviations for Posttest Scores by Levels of Training Type and Management Experience

Variable	Mean	SD
Training Type		
Descriptive ($\underline{N}$ = 42)	5.38	1.79
Prescriptive ($\underline{N}$ = 32)	3.75	1.85
Management Experience:		
Low ($\underline{N}$ = 33)	4.70	2.07
High ($\underline{N}$ = 41)	4.67	1.92

Note. Maximum possible score = 10.00; $\underline{N}$ = 74

PRESENTING TABLES OF GROUP MEANS AND OTHER GROUP DESCRIPTIVE STATISTICS

In addition to the presentation of tables containing frequency counts and percentages, many analyses will examine group differences on "continuous variables." Continuous variables are those that can be scaled along a continuum from highest to lowest, most favorable to least favorable, healthy to unhealthy, and the like. Most psychological, sociological, political, and educational measures can be considered continuous variables. Examples are self-efficacy, alienation, political conservatism/liberalism, verbal reasoning ability, and a host of attitudes representing agreement-disagreement or approval-disapproval on a variety of issues. While some may argue that many of these variables constitute ordinal measurement, and thus pose problems for the computation of means and inferential statistics requiring at least interval measurement, standard practice is to utilize the techniques we suggest below with these variables. Borgatta and Bohrnstedt (1981) argue that these variables are continuous at the latent level and thus, when other assumptions are met, do not pose serious problems for the social sciences.

When your goal is to compare groups on these variables, the first task will be to present the group descriptive statistics in tabular form. For example, a recent dissertation (Sangster, 1991) examined the ability of a training course to improve managers' decision-making ability under conditions of uncertainty. The means and standard deviations for training type and level of management experience are presented in Table 6.9.

Table 6.10 Means and Standard Deviations of Discriminating Variables by User Category

Discriminating Variables	Users		Nonusers	
	X̄	SD	X̄	SD
No. of "D"s and "F"s	1.57	2.67	0.27	0.85
Grade Level	8.37	1.50	7.69	1.40
Importance of Grades	3.16	0.83	3.41	0.75
Arguing with Teachers	2.16	0.83	1.52	0.73
Absent when Not Sick	2.53	1.07	1.68	0.86
Ever Suspended	0.37	0.50	0.08	0.27
How Often Angry	2.84	1.01	2.24	0.52
Fight or Argue with Family	2.63	1.01	2.20	0.71

Note. N = 475 for all discriminating variables.

Note that Table 6.9 is simple and easy to understand. Level of management experience appears to make a difference, and descriptive training appears to result in higher posttest scores than prescriptive training.

The above strategy for presenting group means may be extended to a larger number of groups and a larger number of dependent variables. For example, another recent dissertation (Richards, 1991) examined 16 variables thought to discriminate drug users from nonusers within secondary schools. For each variable, the mean and standard deviation for users and nonusers was presented (see Table 6.10; we have shortened this table to present only the first 8 variables, the full table contains all 16 variables of interest).

FROM DESCRIPTIVE STATISTICS TO STATISTICAL INFERENCE

The materials above refer primarily to descriptions of results as contained in contingency tables and tables containing means or other descriptive statistics, but have not addressed the question of *statistical inference*. The question of inference addresses whether or not the results can be generalized to the population from which the sample was drawn. In other words, this is the question of whether or not the results are *statistically significant*. Questions regarding whether or not the results are statistically significant usually follow tables describing the results, or are contained within them, but should not precede descriptive summaries. For example, in the bivariate table shown above (Table 6.8), the results seem to indicate that parents are more opposed to abortion than those who are not parents; however, this table does NOT address the question of whether or not these results are statistically significant. This question would probably be addressed with a chi-square test.

To facilitate our understanding of tests of statistical significance and how to present them in tabular form, we follow Tabachnik and Fidell (1989) and conceptualize research questions as comprising four major types: the examination of relationships, the comparison of groups, prediction of group membership, and the discovery of structure. Figure 6.1 presents a table designed to facilitate the choice of an appropriate statistical technique and is adapted from the work of Tabachnik and Fidell. Of course there are other types of research questions, but the purpose here is to present analyses that are likely to examine two of these major research questions, the examination of relationships and the comparison of groups. For example, research that tests the hypothesis that, "The greater the amount of academic self-esteem the higher one's grade point average" would constitute an examination of relationships, while research that examines the hypothesis that, "Drop-outs have lower academic self-esteem than those who complete their education," would constitute a comparison of group differences. It is likely that both of the above hypotheses would be examined within the same dissertation, and each hypothesis would be addressed using a different statistical procedure and presented using a different tabular structure.

HOW TO INTERPRET AND PRESENT THE RESULTS OF ANALYSIS OF VARIANCE (ANOVA)

A frequently presented type of statistical analysis is analysis of variance or ANOVA. This section presents an example of an analysis of variance performed by the Statistical Package for the Social Sciences (SPSS-X) (see Table 6.11). The printout is reviewed and an example of how this information might be presented and discussed in a Results section is provided. In the example, the researcher has examined the effect of two independent variables, age and sex, on one dependent variable, a measure of anxiety, labeled E. Note that

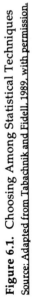

Figure 6.1. Choosing Among Statistical Techniques

Source: Adapted from Tabachnik and Fidell, 1989, with permission.

Table 6.11 <u>Sample SPSS Printout Showing Cell Means and ANOVA Results</u>

```
493 RECODE YRSAGE (60 THRU 74=1) (75 THRU 93=2)
495 ANOVA E BY SEX (1,2) YRSAGE (1,2)
496 STATISTICS 3
                    * * * C E L L   M E A N S * * *
         E <——————————-Dependent Variable
     BY SEX      SUBJECT SEX<——Independent Variable
        YRSAGE   AGE IN YEARS<——-Independent Variable
TOTAL POPULATION
       7.38<——Mean for all 395 subjects (grand mean)
     (  395)<——Number of cases, N
SEX
       1          2<——-There are two categories of sex.
     6.54       8.02<——-Means for each sex
   (  170)   (  225)<——-Number of cases for each sex
YRSAGE
       1          2<——-There are two age categories.
     6.86       8.38<——-Means for each age group
   (  259)   (  136)<——-Number of cases for each age group
           YRSAGE
             1        2   This table represents the full
SEX                       2×2 factorial design.
     1     5.98     7.88
         (  120) (   50)
     2     7.61     8.67
         (  139) (   86)
       * * * A N A L Y S I S   O F   V A R I A N C E * * *
         E<——————-A Measure of Anxiety, The Dependent
                       Variable
       BY  SEX    SUBJECT SEX<——Independent Variable
           YRSAGE  AGE IN YEARS<——-Independent Variable
```

SOURCE OF VARIATION	SUM OF SQUARES	DF	MEAN SQUARE	F	SIGNIF OF F
MAIN EFFECTS	383.382	2	191.691	9.720	.000
SEX	175.938	1	175.938	8.921	.003
YRSAGE	172.247	1	172.247	8.734	.003
2-WAY INTERACTIONS	14.742	1	14.742	.747	.388
SEX YRSAGE	14.742	1	14.742	.747	.388
EXPLAINED	398.124	3	132.708	6.729	.000
RESIDUAL	7711.152	391	19.722		
TOTAL	8109.276	394	20.582		

```
395 CASES WERE PROCESSED.  0 CASES ( .0 PCT) WERE MISSING.
```

Table 6.12 <u>Mean Anxiety Scores by Age and Sex</u>

	Age	
	60-74	*75-93*
Sex		
Male	5.98	7.88
	(120)	(50)
Female	7.61	8.67
	(139)	(86)

<u>Note</u>. <u>N</u>s in parentheses.

anything <u>underlined</u> is not part of the printout, but represents explanatory material that we have added.

The three numbered lines directly below the caption in Table 6.11 are the lines of code (instructions) that directed SPSS-X to perform the analysis. The first line (RECODE) divides the age variable into two groups, the young-old, including those between 60 and 74, and the old-old, containing all those 75 to 93. The second line (ANOVA) contains the name of the statistical procedure and the variables upon which analysis of variance is to be conducted. The third line (STATISTICS) provides the number of an additional statistic that is desired in addition to the actual analysis of variance table. In this case the "3" instructs the program to include the cell means with the other results.

The SPSS printout in Table 6.11 is quite different from what one sees in a dissertation table. We have chosen to present these results as tables. Table 6.12 presents the means of the full 2 × 2 factorial design. Table 6.13 presents the ANOVA results. Note that in both tables we have replaced the "Variable Names" used by the computer with the complete name of the variable that a reader can understand. In other words, "E" has become "Anxiety," and "YRSAGE" has become "Age." Each category has been given its appropriate label, Male and Female for the Sex variable (not 1 and 2), and 60-74 and 75-93 for the Age variable (not 1 and 2).

Table 6.12 shows that males generally have lower anxiety than females and that the old-old have generally higher anxiety than the young-old. Table 6.13 presents the results of the statistical tests of the effect of age, the effect of sex, and the interaction of age and sex on anxiety. Note that in Table 6.13 not all of the information from the ANOVA table in the printout was presented. This is because computer printouts print information that is often redundant in one analysis, but

Table 6.13 Analysis of Variance of Anxiety Scores by Age and Sex

SOURCE	SS	DF	MS	F
SEX	175.9	1	175.9	8.9*
AGE	172.2	1	172.2	8.7*
SEX × AGE	14.7	1	14.7	0.7
RESIDUAL	7711.2	391	19.7	
TOTAL	8074.0	394	20.6	

* $p < .01$

not redundant in others. We have eliminated the rows labeled "MAIN EFFECTS, 2 WAY INTERACTIONS" and "EXPLAINED" because they are not necessary in this example. The column labeled "SIGNIFICANCE OF F" has been eliminated because it is handled by the probability note indicating the significance level of the F values at the bottom of the table.

Finally, after building your tables, you will need to describe them within the text. This is particularly important because the tables are intended to elaborate upon the text, not substitute for it. The text needs to stand on its own as a focus for the reader in summarizing the results of the research. We use the sample statement types discussed earlier in the section on "The Nuts and Bolts of Describing Quantitative Results" to describe Tables 6.12 and 6.13.

> Table 6.12 presents the mean anxiety scores by age and sex. Overall, females have higher anxiety levels than males and the old-old have higher anxiety levels than young-old. An analysis of variance of these results is presented in Table 6.13. Both the age and sex main effects were statistically significant. For sex, $F(1, 391) = 8.92$, $p < .01$, and for age $F(1, 391) = 8.72$, $p < .01$. The interaction effect between age and sex was not statistically significant.

STREAMLINING YOUR RESULTS: PRESENTING MULTIPLE ANALYSES IN A SINGLE TABLE

It is frequently the case that many similar analyses may need to be presented in a Results section. For example, if the study described in the previous section had also examined the relationship of sex and age on depression, locus of control, and four dimensions of life satisfaction, each of these analyses would also need to be presented in tabular form. If each set of means and each ANOVA summary table were presented in separate tables, an additional 12 tables would be necessary. When such a situation arises we strongly recommend that you seek a means by which the results may be combined into a single table. For example, a student of ours (Paape, 1992) examined the relationship of five health locus of control subtypes and seven variables related to health values and behaviors. Her hypotheses suggest that certain subtypes practice more healthy behaviors and value health more. In this study one-way analysis of variance was used to examine the differences between the five health locus of control subtypes and the multiple dependent variables. Rather than present each of the seven analyses in separate tables she decided to combine them into a single table as shown in Table 6.14.

Note that Table 6.14 presents the mean, standard deviation, and number of cases for each variable for each health locus of control subtype, but does not present the complete ANOVA summary table for each analysis. It is sufficient to present only the F ratio and the accompanying probability notes (or exact probability value in some cases) to indicate the statistical significance of each analysis. Such a presentation enables the reader to examine all of the results related to specific research questions in a single table, facilitating discussion and comprehension of the results.

As a second example, consider the situation in which one or more groups are asked a number of questions in conjunction with follow-up questions. You may want to present the answers to both the main questions and the follow-ups for each group in the study. An efficient way to do this is to present the results in a table that facilitates the examination of the questions and comparisons between groups. For example, in a study of marriage, child, and family counselors, and psychologists, Neighbors (1991) asked each to rate the courses they had taken in the diagnosis, etiology, and physiology of mental disorder. Each area was rated as "not adequate," "adequate," or "very adequate." Following these ratings the same groups were asked to rate their need for additional education in each area. Ratings were coded "yes" to indicate the perceived need for more education. A "no" response indicated no perceived need for additional training. Tables that present bivariate distributions such as these were discussed in an earlier section. A bivariate distribution could be presented for each area of training and each assessment of the need for

Table 6.14 <u>Analysis of Variance of Health Values and Risk Mix by Health Locus of Control Subtypes</u>

Variable	I	II	III	Type IV	V	F
Health Value						2.71*
Mean	2.9	2.1	3.0	2.6	2.4	
S.D.	2.2	1.5	2.2	2.2	1.7	
N	133	57	105	112	113	
Risk-Mix						3.25*
Mean	2.6	3.1	2.3	2.5	2.9	
S.D.	1.5	2.2	1.3	1.7	1.6	
N	133	57	105	113	113	
Smoking						0.52
Mean	2.0	2.1	1.9	2.0	2.1	
S.D.	1.1	0.9	1.1	0.9	0.9	
N	133	57	105	113	113	
Sleep						0.81
Mean	1.7	1.7	1.7	1.6	1.7	
S.D.	0.6	0.5	0.6	0.7	0.5	
N	133	57	105	113	113	
Weight						1.19
Mean	0.7	0.6	0.7	0.6	0.6	
S.D.	0.5	0.5	0.5	0.5	0.5	
N	133	57	105	113	113	
Diet						1.04
Mean	4.5	4.6	4.3	4.2	4.5	
S.D.	1.5	1.3	1.4	1.5	1.5	
N	133	57	105	113	113	
Habits						4.28*
Mean	2.9	3.5	2.8	3.2	3.2	
S.D.	1.2	1.0	1.3	1.2	1.2	
N	133	57	105	113	113	

Note. I = Pure Internal, II = Pure Powerful Others, III = Pure Chance, IV = Double External, V = Believer in Control.
*$p < .05$

more training, making a total of six tables. The statistical significance of each relationship was assessed with a chi-square test, creating a need to present the results of these tests also. Table 6.15 presents the results of the above analyses in a single table. Note that Table 6.15 presents the data for both questions, for each group, in a single row. Only the percentage who gave a positive (yes) response to the question regarding the need for more education is presented because the percentage who stated "no" is redundant, obtained simply by

Table 6.15 <u>Self-Ratings of Adequacy of Education and Need for More Education</u>
<u>by Type of License</u>

| Type of Course | Adequacy of Education(%) | | | Need More | |
	Not Adequate	Adequate	Very Adequate	% "Yes"	χ^2 (df, N)
Diagnosis					
Psychologists	48.2	25.9	25.9(27)	35.9(40)	6.9(2, 76)*
MFCCs	26.5	57.2	16.3(49)	29.8(57)	0.3(1, 97)
Etiology					
Psychologists	38.5	42.3	19.2(26)	30.0(40)	3.9(2, 73)
MFCCs	21.3	65.9	12.8(47)	24.6(57)	0.4(1, 97)
Physiology					
Psychologists	36.0	28.0	36.0(25)	42.5(40)	3.5(2, 72)
MFCCs	40.4	42.6	17.0(47)	42.1(57)	0.0(1, 97)

<u>Notes</u>. Cell percentages for "Adequacy of Education" sum to 100 across columns. <u>N</u>s in parentheses. The first chi-square value represents "Adequacy of Education," the second represents "Need for More Education."
*p < .05

subtracting the percentage who said yes from 100. The chi-square tests, one for each question, are presented in the column labeled χ^2. A general note indicates that the first chi-square value represents the test for the adequacy of education question, while the second presents the test for the need for more education question.

As a final caution, it is important to point out that one can carry the quest to streamline tables too far. The result is considerable confusion rather than clarification and ease of comparison. Table 6.15 may be approaching the limits in this regard, but we believe that it presents a strategy for approaching table construction that will be useful to students.

PRESENTING CORRELATION ANALYSES AND CORRELATION MATRICES

Correlations express the degree of relationship between two variables and are often calculated in dissertations that examine relationships between variables. When only a few correlations are calculated these may not require the use of a table. Such relationships can be described in the text by statements of the following type. "The

Table 6.16 <u>Means, Standard Deviations and Correlations of Variables X, Y, and Z</u>

	X	Y	Z
X	1.00		
Y	0.25	1.00	
Z	0.01	0.35	1.0
X̄	3.61	2.74	4.10
S	1.23	1.66	0.93

relationship between age of youngest child and number of hours worked by all women in the sample was negative and statistically significant ($\underline{r}(75) = -.21$, $\underline{p} < .01$)." The statement in parentheses indicates both the strength of the relationship (.21, a weak to moderate relationship) and its statistical significance (significant at less than .01). The 75 in parentheses following the underlined r is the degrees of freedom associated with the statistical test and is one less than the sample size (i.e., $N - 1$).

When a large number of relationships are examined simultaneously it may be necessary to present the *correlation matrix* in a table. Two examples are given. The first represents a hypothetical analysis examining the relationship between three variables, X, Y, and Z. Note that it is standard to present the means and standard deviations of all variables in an analysis along with their correlations. We have included these with the correlation matrix of X, Y, and Z in Table 6.16.

Note that Table 6.16 contains only the correlations below the diagonal of 1.0s. This is because correlations are *symmetrical*, that is, the correlation of X with Z is identical to the correlation of Z with X. Thus there is no need to present both the lower and upper diagonal. Note also that the 1.0s on the "main diagonal" represent the correlation of a variable with itself. These values are always 1.0.

A second example is derived from a recent article by Rogers, Parcel, and Menaghan (1991) examining the relationship between mother's work and child behavior problems. Rogers et al. presented the correlation matrix of 23 variables (253 unique correlations) in a single table. We present only the first 5 of these variables in Table 6.17.

A number of variations of the tables discussed above may be encountered in the literature and used by the student. First, the decimal points may be eliminated as they are usually assumed to exist with correlation coefficients. Second, the main diagonal of ones

Table 6.17 Means, Standard Deviations, and Correlations for Mother's Work and Child Behavior Problems (Rogers, Parcel, & Menaghan, 1991)

	1	2	3	4	5
1 Behavior Problems	1.0				
2 Mastery	−.18	1.0			
3 Maternal Education	−.08	.21	1.0		
4 Child's Age	−.05	−.03	−.11	1.0	
5 Hourly Pay	−.10	.19	.24	.02	1.0
X̄	−.80	.27	2.07	62.51	5.58
S	11.41	12.38	1.48	10.15	2.87

Note. Correlations of .08 or greater are significant when one-tailed tests are used.

is sometimes used to present the standard deviations, as opposed to presenting these in a separate row below the correlations as has been shown here. Third, the correlations may be asterisked and probability notes may be used. Fourth, the number of cases may be included in a note, or, when there is much variation from value to value, may be placed in parentheses below each correlation.

PRESENTING THE RESULTS OF MULTIPLE REGRESSION ANALYSIS

Multiple Regression Analysis (MRA) is a multivariate statistical technique that examines the relationship between continuously distributed independent variables and one continuously distributed dependent variable. In contrast to ANOVA presentations, there appears to be no standard, universally agreed upon format in which to present the results of MRA. This is not particularly surprising, given the many variations of MRA available and the complexity of the models being tested. Many of our students have used MRA in recent dissertations and all have struggled with both the interpretation and presentation of the results. In this section we make some suggestions and present a few examples that may be used as guides.

A wide variety of output may be generated by multiple regression analysis programs. This includes, but is not limited to, unstandardized and standardized regression coefficients (also known as "beta weights"), multiple correlations and their square (R squared or R^2)

Table 6.18 Sample Table for Presenting the Results of Multiple Regression Analysis, Three Independent Variables

Independent Variable	B	Beta	t
Variable 1			
Variable 2			
Variable 3			
$R^2 =$, $F =$			

*p < .05.**p < .01.***p < .001.

and changes in the values of R and/or R^2 in stepwise regression procedures. In addition to these statistics, there will usually be t and F statistics indicating the statistical significance of these various coefficients. We offer Table 6.18 as a model table to be used in describing the results of MRA.

Table 6.18 presents the independent variables in the rows and the regression coefficients, unstandardized (B) and standardized (Beta) in the columns. The t values associated with the regression coefficients are also presented in the columns. The R^2 value is presented at the bottom of the column, with its associated F ratio. The t values and F value would be asterisked if statistically significant at the specified level.

AN EXAMPLE OF
MULTIPLE REGRESSION ANALYSIS

For example, imagine a study examining the effects of education, age, and frequency of church attendance on attitudes toward premarital sex. (Clearly there are other variables that could also influence these attitudes, but we want to keep this example simple.) Table 6.19 presents the results of a multiple regression analysis examining the effect of these variables. The results are based on data from the 1990 NORC General Social Survey.

Table 6.19 presents the standardized and unstandardized regression coefficients and their accompanying t-values. Note that, as indicated by the probability notes, all t-values are statistically significant at $p < .001$. The beta weights provide an indication of the relative contribution of the variables to the prediction of attitudes toward premarital sex, when the other variables are controlled. Clearly, church attendance has the greatest influence, followed by

Table 6.19 Multiple Regression Analysis of Attitudes Toward Premarital Sexual Relations on Education, Age, and Frequency of Church Attendance

Independent Variable	B	Beta	t
Education	0.05	0.12	4.06*
Age	−0.02	−0.23	−7.50*
Attendance	−0.18	−0.39	−13.00*
R^2 = .25, F(2, 435) = 97.00*			

*p < .001

age and education. The R^2 indicates that 25% of the variance in attitudes toward premarital sex can be explained by the combined influence of the three independent variables. Note that this value, as indicated by an F value, is also statistically significant.

PRESENTING THE RESULTS
OF QUALITATIVE RESEARCH

Naturalistic inquiry is likely to produce large quantities of data that represent words and ideas rather than numbers and statistics. These include, but are not limited to, interview transcripts and field notes, a wide variety of records, documents, and unobtrusive measures. The researcher may be the victim of "data overload," with no idea of what to present or where to begin. The task of "data reduction" is part and parcel of quantitative analysis, but "the art of naturalistic data processing is far from well developed" (Lincoln & Guba, 1985, p. 354). While statistical program packages, such as SPSS, SAS, and BMDP present data in standardized ways that permit immediate comparisons both within and across groups, each qualitative analysis requires the researcher to devise his or her own method for presenting the results.

Despite some disagreements about method, both quantitative and qualitative researchers agree that the primary issue is making sense of the data. According to Lincoln and Guba, "What is at issue is the best means to 'make sense' of the data in ways that will facilitate the continuing unfolding of the inquiry, and, second, lead to a maximal understanding (in the sense of *verstehen*) of the phenomenon being studied" (Lincoln & Guba, 1985, p. 224). Making sense of the data in the naturalistic sense means processing the data through some technique of inductive analysis. One approach involves two essential subprocesses that compose the basis of inductive analysis, unitizing and categorizing. *Unitizing* is essentially a coding operation that identifies information units isolated from the text. In the second subprocess, *categorizing,* information units derived from the unitizing phase are organized into categories on the basis of similarity in meaning. As the number of categories reaches a saturation point the researcher attempts to write rules that define which units of information may be included or excluded from the category. This process is called the "constant comparative method" by Glaser and Strauss (1967). The constant comparative method requires continual revision, modification, and amendment until all new units can be placed into an appropriate category and the inclusion of additional units into a category provides no new information.

For example, Dumas (1989) examined the relationship between daughters and fathers in family-owned businesses. She describes her data analysis as follows:

> Data analysis for each family-business interviewed consisted of unitizing and categorizing the data collected during 40 indepth interviews averaging 2.5 hours each. I categorized these units in an ongoing manner by provisionally categorizing the cards (units) that seemed to relate to the same content. As I did this, I devised propositional statements to characterize each category's properties. I then combined these properties into rules for inclusion in each category. These rules served to justify the inclusion of each card which ultimately remained assigned to a category, to render each category set internally consistent. I then gave each category a title which was an attempt to capture the essence of the rule for inclusion of units in the category. Finally, I reviewed the entire set of categories I had formulated, including the miscellaneous cards. Some of these were eventually discarded as irrelevant. To determine when it was time to stop collecting and processing data, I used the four criteria proposed by Lincoln and Guba (1985): exhaustion of sources; saturation of categories . . . emergence of regularities . . . and overextension. (pp. 207-209)

Dumas found seven constructs that describe the essence of her interviews with fathers and daughters in family-owned businesses. She describes these constructs as, "intended to portray the situations studied, and to make the complexities of each situation apparent, as well as indicate how these complexities interact." For example, construct one, "Daddy's Little Girl," refers to the "roles assigned to the daughters by their fathers and the daughters themselves." According to Dumas:

> These fathers and daughters had no previous point of reference for how to behave when working together. They only had their previous roles of father and daughter as models for how to relate to each other. Therefore the fathers and daughters interviewed often found working together confusing, unsettling and stressful. As these daughters indicated:

> Even though I've been here a long time I still have to kiss him every morning. Otherwise he'll be hurt. I don't think he's made the transition to seeing me as an adult. I'm still his little girl.

> I never know whether I'm talking to my dad or my boss! It drives me crazy! My dad too. I just don't know when he expects me to be "daddy's little girl" and when he expects me to be businesslike. That makes it hard on me. (p. 237)

The work of Dumas illustrates how the results of qualitative analysis may be reported. Following a conceptual definition of the meaning of a category, relevant quotes that illustrate this meaning are presented. While some authors take the position that a case study report is primarily written, others, such as Miles and Huberman (1984), suggest that the use of a wide variety of displays, presenting one's conceptual framework, context of analysis, and results, greatly facilitates the analysis of qualitative data. They provide advice on constructing scatterplots, context charts, causal networks, and causal models. Our students have generally chosen to utilize a combination of techniques to present their results, including written, graphic, and tabular displays.

It is important for the qualitative researcher to describe the "context" in which a particular event takes place. Miles and Huberman suggest the "context chart" as one manner in which to do this. The context chart, "maps in graphic form the interrelationships among the roles, groups (and, if appropriate, organizations) that go to make up the context of individual behavior" (Miles & Huberman, 1984, p. 92). For example, in addition to illustrating the meaning of each construct developed in her analysis, as quoted above, Dumas (1989) also presented a "genogram" and "organization chart" for each family business included in her research. The genogram (see Figure 6.2) presented the family tree as a guide to locating each interviewee's position in the family, while the organization chart (see Figure 6.3)

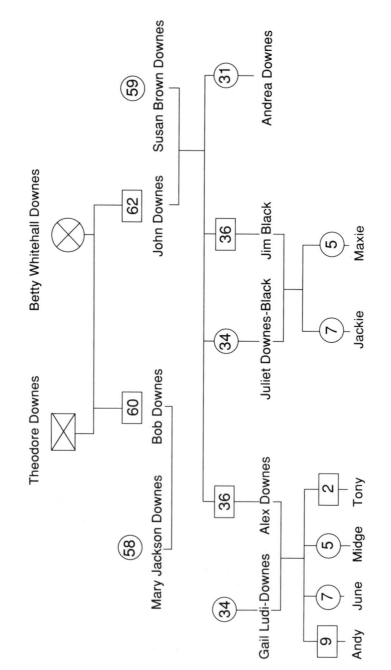

Figure 6.2. Downes Family Genogram
Source: From Dumas, 1989. Used with permission.

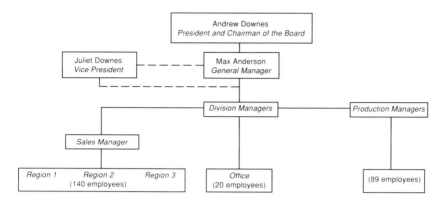

Figure 6.3. Downes, Inc. Organization Chart
Source. Dumas (1989). Used with permission.

depicted each interviewee's position in the family business. As a second example, Leon (1991) studied motivation for gang membership among Anglo and Hispanic incarcerated juveniles. Table 6.20 presents a matrix designed to classify descriptions provided by gang members as to reasons for joining a gang. This table is based on the suggestion of Miles and Huberman (1984) to build a matrix display that "blocks descriptive data segments around a particular event or experience."

This matrix has been completed with a summary statement (an exact quote could also have been used) that represents the reasons given by each participant, represented by a letter indicating their ethnicity (H or W) and an identification number (1, 2, 3, etc.) that placed the participant in the respective row.

Table 6.20 Reasons for Joining a Gang for White and Hispanic Gang Members

Participants	Reasons
Hispanics	
H1	Grew up with it
H2	All my friends part of it
H3	Grew up with it
Whites	
W1	All my friends part of it
W2	Fun
W3	Hanging out

A *causal network* is a graph displaying the independent and dependent variables in a naturalistic study. Such a graph uses arrows to represent the direction of influence (causality) and makes specific notations regarding the meaning of the connections between the arrows linking the variables in the analysis. This chart may serve as the basis for a conceptual framework or the development of "grounded" theory. For example, Williams (1989) examined the transition from individualism to social advocacy as experienced by 13 American social advocates. The descriptive model Williams developed from an analysis of interviews contained what Williams called "turning points." As Williams (p. 240) states, "The advocates often reflected upon significant 'markers' in their transitions and how the role of self-directed action at those markers influenced the course of the transition." Figure 6.4 contains Williams's representation of "marking the course," in the transition from individualism to social advocacy.

In sum, both qualitative and quantitative analyses pose the same task for the researcher, "making sense" of the data. The methods of analyses may differ, the standards upon which reliability and validity are judged may not be the same, and the raw data upon which analysis is based assumes very different forms. Nevertheless, clearly written and documented analytical summaries, the use of tables and graphs, and a careful consideration of the order and logic of presentation serves as the foundation of quality research, regardless of the researcher's method of choice.

NOTE

1. The four statements for describing quantitative results were suggested by Dr. David Perkins, Department of Psychology, California State University, Fullerton.

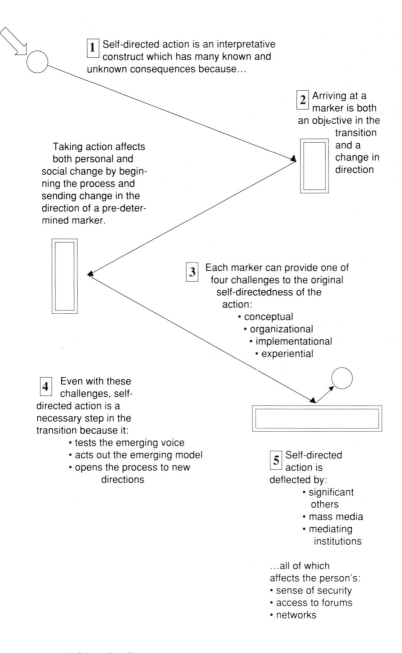

Figure 6.4. Marking the Course
Source. Williams (1989). Used with permission.

Box 6.1

STUDENT SUGGESTIONS

1. Anticipate how answers will be coded and analyzed from questionnaires. Figure out how many computer card columns you will need to transfer the data. Be sure to allow enough columns for the longest possible response.

2. Many students hire consultants to help them analyze their data. Doing research is more expensive than I ever imagined! One way to cut the expense of a statistical consultant is to enter the coding of responses on a computer disk yourself. A computer consultant can run the actual program for relatively little expense. Always stay on top of what the consultant is doing to your data!

3. Most statistical analyses can be done on personal computers these days. One advantage of not relying on a mainframe for analyzing your data is that it, or the person who has access to it, may not always be available to you. If you use a program written for a home computer you can always go back to your data for some reanalysis or further analysis that your committee requests.

7 ✔

Discussion

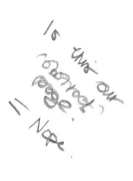

By the time data have been collected and analyzed and the Results chapter of the dissertation has been completed, proceeding to write the remainder of the dissertation may seem anticlimactic. Consequently, many students do not do justice to the Discussion chapter and it ends up being less thoughtful and comprehensive than it should be.

The Discussion chapter is an opportunity to move beyond the data and integrate creatively the results of your study with existing theory and research. Whereas clear guidelines exist for preparing a Method chapter and Results chapter in terms of content and format, no such formal guidelines exist for writing the Discussion chapter. A good Discussion chapter typically contains the following elements:

1. An overview of the significant findings of the study
2. A consideration of the findings in light of existing research studies
3. Implications of the study for current theory (except in purely applied studies)
4. A careful examination of findings that fail to support or only partially support your hypotheses
5. Limitations of the study that may affect the validity or the generalizability of the results
6. Recommendations for further research
7. Implications of the study for professional practice or applied settings (optional)

Think back to the research wheel introduced in Chapter 1, which describes how the dissertation process is an evolving shift between deductive and inductive modes of reasoning, from the general to the specific and back again to the general. The Discussion chapter is largely an exercise in inductive thinking, grappling with the specific results of your study and drawing inferences to the world of theory by linking your results with the existing literature. This chapter takes over where the introduction and review of the literature left off and may be quite similar to it in style and content. Here you are forwarding your conceptual argument on the basis of the obtained data, exploring the meaning of the data from the relationships that have emerged among the variables of the study. You evaluate the extent to which your study answered the questions you posed at the outset, basing your reasoning as much as possible on the data themselves. As you marshall your own interpretation of the findings, consider the strengths and weaknesses of alternative interpretations from the literature, and the points of agreement and disagreement between your data and conclusions in comparison with the contributions of others. A good Discussion chapter openly acknowledges and evaluates rival explanations for the results.

It is not sufficient to reiterate the findings of your study, although this is a good place to begin. One popular way of starting the chapter is by reviewing, in turn, the status of each of the hypotheses and research questions of the study now that the data have been collected and examined. Stay focused on a straightforward exposition of what you determined, taking the principal ideas one at a time. In so doing, avoid terminology that is meaningless outside of the context of your study, such as referring to "hypothesis number one" or noting that "the A group scored significantly higher than the B group." Instead, use plain English and refer to the variables by name so that readers unfamiliar with the specific terminology of your study will be able to comprehend the meaning of the results. For example, the following sentence is an accurate restatement of a finding that may have been expressed more technically in the Results chapter: "The teachers who received intensive training in conflict resolution skills were significantly more successful in defusing classroom conflicts than teachers without such training."

Perhaps the most common oversight made in writing the Discussion chapter is a failure to return to the literature to integrate results of the study with other empirical studies examining the same phenomena. A good discussion embeds each result within the theoretical context that was presented in the literature review. Thus you will need to cite some of the relevant studies that were previously discussed, as well as return to the literature to seek additional ways of understanding your results and look for confirmatory or disconfirmatory evidence. The kinds of statements that are often found in Discussion chapters are of the following form:

> The results of this study are consistent with Jones's findings of a negative relationship between learned helplessness and efforts to seek employment and extends his findings to a nonhandicapped population.

> Unlike Smith (1989), who relied upon self-report to look for evidence of dissimulation, the current study found behavioral evidence that teenagers drink more alcohol than they admit to family members.

Here are some other suggestions for writing an appropriate Discussion chapter, based on common misunderstandings:

1. The data analyses should have been thoroughly presented in the Results chapter. In the same way that findings are not discussed in the Results chapter, secondary analyses of data are not presented in the Discussion chapter.

2. Don't repeat and reformulate points that have already been made. This chapter is frequently regarded as a summary of specific findings. On the contrary, discuss the findings rather than describe them again. Focus on explaining how your data can be used to infer broader conceptual and theoretical statements by analyzing the relationships among your specific variables. An example of such a generalized statement might be, "On the basis of these findings, it appears that loss of a parent leads to an increased risk of adolescent suicidal behavior only in those families that fail to communicate openly about their grief." Avoid speculation that is not related to empirical data or theory.

3. A common tendency among students is to list all possible criticisms of a study and to do so with an apologetic tone. It is much better to accept the study for what it is. If there are fundamental criticisms, such as attributing negative findings to a major flaw in the design of the study, it is reasonable to question why the study was conducted in the first place. At the same time, it is not unreasonable to identify flaws that were unintended or were delimitations in

the study. But do so only in the context of evaluating the relative trustworthiness of your conclusions.

4. A parallel tendency is to offer a long list of recommendations for future research. This is inadvisable. It is much better to focus on one or two major recommendations. For example, to suggest that a study be extended to males, to brunettes, to 13- to 16-year-olds, and so on, is a waste of space. It is preferable to suggest the next reasonable step in forwarding a program of research in a given area of study.

5. Be careful not to offer suggestions for future research that can be easily addressed within your own study. These only indicate that you have not done a thorough job of examining your own data.

6. Don't include trivial details or ramble aimlessly around the topic. This is an opportunity to think creatively, but as with all other chapters of the dissertation, the Discussion chapter should also be logical and focused. One specific way to maintain the balanced perspective of the scientific investigator is to avoid melodramatic or intemperate language, such as "amazing," or even "interesting" or "important." Allow your data and conclusions to be judged on their own merits and not on your amplification of them.

The mandate to present and discuss significant findings is clear. What do you do, however, when results are not statistically significant or "nearly" significant? One cannot pretend that a nonsignificant finding is significant and, strictly speaking, it should not be treated as such. On the other hand, conventions regarding significance levels (e.g., .05, .01) are somewhat arbitrary, and each field seems to have its own prevailing standards for acknowledging or ignoring trends that do not quite live up to these a priori levels. Our own position is that the size of a finding, expressed, for example, in the percentage of variance accounted for between two variables, is ultimately more informative than the presence or absence of a statistically significant effect. This is another reason not to be blinded by statistics, either in terms of overestimating or underestimating the meaning of a particular result.

Students may become particularly disheartened with nonsignificant results, when hypotheses are not validated. But nonsignificant results need not imply an inferior study. The research enterprise is a treasure hunt with an unknown outcome, and if a study is performed according to acceptable standards, negative results ought not invalidate the legitimacy of the research. Prior to collecting data it is important to anticipate how to explain the full range of empirical outcomes so that no result will be a bad result. Any result should be conceptually informative, in the sense of forwarding knowledge in a field. Negative results should, however, signal the need for a complete inquiry. Such results can typically be attributed to methodological shortcomings or a theoretical critique. An opportunity to challenge commonly understood theory can serve as a major research contribution. Methodological shortcomings may be more difficult to handle, since it is presumed that they would have been attended to in designing the study. Nonetheless, there is usually some disparity between the best laid plans and real world events. Even the most meticulous researcher may not correctly anticipate mailings that go awry, research assistants who quit, subjects who refuse to complete a posttest, and equipment that malfunctions.

Dissertations do not typically contain a Summary section, although a subheading entitled "Conclusions" is not unusual. This is the place to summarize concisely the principal implications of your findings in a few paragraphs. Resist the temptation to use the final pages of the dissertation as a pulpit to lament the sorry state of affairs in your area of study, your discipline, or the world at large, or conversely, to rhapsodize about the terrific opportunities afforded to anyone willing or able to capitalize on the significance of your study. An inspired quotation or eloquent turn of phrase can add a nice touch to the conclusion, but there is a difference between forceful writing and gratuitous clichés.

ABSTRACT

Every dissertation requires an Abstract, which is essentially a brief summary of the project and is placed before the introductory chapter. The clarity of the abstract should not be overlooked because it is this section of the dissertation that is generally reproduced in computerized data bases as well as in Dissertation Abstracts. It is also the section of the dissertation that is usually read first and may be the only section that is read. Thus the abstract should accurately reflect the content of the dissertation and be written in a way that makes the study seem articulate and scholarly.

It is relatively easy to put together a good abstract after a dissertation is completed. You can almost lift two or three key sentences from each chapter of the dissertation to assemble the abstract, because the abstract needs to provide an overview of the study's purpose, method, results, and implications. It is important to be precise and specific and not include content that is not present in the dissertation itself. Dissertation abstracts are generally about 150 words in length and include short statements summarizing the research problem, the subjects, the method and procedures (avoiding abbreviations and idiosyncratic terms), the results, and the conclusions and implications. Write in the past tense to report specific manipulations and procedures you employed in the study and the present tense to describe conclusions based on the findings. Here is a sample abstract based on a recent dissertation (Wegmann, 1992):

> This study carries forward the exploration of a link between authoritarianism and deficits in cognitive functioning. The subjects were 50 community college students and 29 registered voters recently assigned to jury duty. All participants completed Altemeyer's Right-Wing Authoritarianism Scale and three early-stage information processing tasks: 1) content recognition of a news article two minutes after exposure; 2) content recognition of a recorded debate two minutes after exposure, and 3) the selection of correct inferential statements in a set of brief paragraphs taken from the Watson & Glasser Critical Thinking Appraisal Test. The experimental setting utilized a computer laboratory with an interactive program that guided and monitored each subject through all phases of the study.
>
> When the acquisition of new material was in written format, authoritarianism interacted with reading skills to limit the recognition and retention of new information. When new material was presented orally, retention was significantly impacted by authoritarianism. Subjects in both samples who scored high in authoritarianism also made significantly more inferential errors. The data strongly suggest that authoritarianism covaries significantly with a lessened ability to process incoming cognitive information with reasonable care and accuracy.

TITLE

It may seem strange to position a statement about writing a title of the dissertation in the last chapter. Dissertations often have working titles that are amended when the study is completed. We are frequently amazed at how little attention students give to composing a clear and accurate title. This is in spite of the fact that the title is the vehicle that carries the meaning of the dissertation into the professional community. In constructing a title, remember to:

1. Include all necessary key words to correctly and fully convey the content of the study.
2. Delete all words that are redundant or do not contribute to the essential meaning.
3. Order the words to reflect accurately the meaning you intend.

Here are some examples of titles that are problematic:

A study of information processing deficits of the authoritarian personality. The phrase "A study of" is redundant and unnecessary. Better: *Information processing deficits of the authoritarian personality.*

The effect of sexually abused children testifying in court. The word order makes it unclear who is being affected by the testimony. An alternative order: *The effect of testifying in court on sexually abused children.*

An exploratory study of the interrelationship of loneliness, obesity, and other selected variables within two of Bruch's obesity subgroups and a control group. Much too long and cumbersome. Try to reduce your title to 12-15 key words that summarize the main idea. For example: *The role of loneliness in Bruch's obesity subgroups.*

Predicting acting-out behavior from the achromatic-chromatic HTP. Do not use abbreviations in the title. Accurate indexing of the dissertation depends upon writing out all variables. Better: *Predicting acting-out behavior from the achromatic-chromatic House-Tree-Person Test.*

Box 7.1

STUDENT SUGGESTIONS

1. You can't always rely on standard manuscript and publication guides to give you the exact format needed for your dissertation. Since dissertations are submitted to your graduate school, and not to a journal, you will need to consult your program's requirements for preparing the final manuscript. There seem to be departmental differences, for example, on whether or not to include a Summary, whether or not to include applications in the Discussion chapter, and how to format references.

2. It was tempting to think of my dissertation as finished when the data were collected and analyzed. I had to get my second wind to write the Discussion chapter. I recommend allotting sufficient time and energy to think about the meaning and implication of your results. Don't set unrealistic deadlines for completing this chapter! In many ways it becomes the most important chapter of the dissertation.

PART III

Working With Process: What You Need to Know to Make the Dissertation Easier

Overcoming Barriers:
Becoming an Expert While
Controlling Your Own Destiny

Throughout this book we have interspersed firsthand suggestions from some of our students to streamline the task of completing the dissertation successfully. In this chapter we take up six specific types of issues that, when unattended, can lead to complications in the dissertation process. They are: working with your committee; emotional blocks; task blocks; getting organized; depending upon others for data collection and data analysis; dissertation orals. Awareness of these issues can go a long way toward the prevention of subsequent trouble.

WORKING WITH YOUR COMMITTEE

Each dissertation committee becomes its own social system. Under the best circumstances all of the committee members work together smoothly, communicate frequently, and support the student through the dissertation process. That's the ideal scenario. In real life things rarely happen so fortuitously. Committee members disagree and squabble, each member has his or her personal axe to grind, and at

131

least one recalcitrant or neglectful member holds up the completion
of the dissertation in an inexcusable fashion.

Students in most graduate programs have the opportunity to
choose most, if not all, of their committee members. Certainly the
rumor mill in most academic departments provides enough data
about this selection process. It may be tempting for you to choose
"easy" committee members, that is, faculty who may let you get
away with an inferior product and not offer much in the way of
feedback—helpful or not. In our experience there is little advantage
in avoiding difficult committee members, if by *difficult* one means,
not obstinate or unreasonable, but those who give rigorous feedback
and demand the highest quality product. We have found that students who are willing to invite, insist upon, and manage thorough,
sometimes critical, feedback early in the dissertation process, end up
not only with superior studies, but with proposals that glide smoothly
through almost any knowledgeable reader's hands in the later stages.
The way to get through many challenging educational hurdles, as
well as situations in life, is being able to manage negative feedback
with grace and nondefensiveness. It is a skill worth cultivating.

We would be remiss, however, if we did not note that one can
cogently argue for choosing a very competent and supportive chair,
working closely with that person, and selecting additional committee members who are not likely to provide much substantive input
and, hence, slow down the dissertation process! With this cynical but
possibly pragmatic strategy, you would be encouraged to circulate
drafts of the dissertation to committee members as infrequently as
possible and rely on the wisdom and support of your chairperson
for major input and guidance. Whether or not this strategy seems
appropriate should depend in part upon your assessment of the
political climate of your department.

One aspect of the skill of managing feedback is how to deal with
instances when committee members differ among themselves and
make contradictory recommendations. Certainly faculty have their
own tastes and preferences and vested interests. One committee
member suggests using a particular scale while a second committee
member nominates another scale; one person says to delete a section
while another person says to expand it. This is to be expected, and
no committee will ever be in total agreement. You need to stay in
charge of your own project and negotiate with each faculty member.
It is vital to know which suggestions are critical and which are
window dressing. There is no point in being obstinate about making

minor changes to please someone who possesses a vote on your academic future. At the same time you need to maintain your integrity on important issues and argue them persuasively, based on facts and logic, not emotional resistance. When committee members have divergent opinions that seem nonnegotiable, it is time to appeal to your chairperson for support and perhaps to turn the dilemma over to the faculty themselves to resolve. Never, however, play faculty against one another.

The constitution of the committee is significant. Always begin by selecting a chairperson and then consulting with your chair before inviting the other members. All faculty have a "short list" of colleagues they either enjoy working with or abhor working with. In a general sense, you want committee members who will promote rather than hinder your progress. Beyond this universal guideline, one way to think about the composition of a dissertation or thesis committee is in terms of the roles the participants play. If your study concerns the fears of Asian immigrant children, it makes sense to have at least one committee member representing expertise in each of the major variables: fears, phobias, or anxieties; Asian culture and immigration; children or developmental issues. If you are fortunate, all of these characteristics may be wrapped up in one or two persons (such as when a study is derived from a faculty mentor's ongoing research program), but it may require three distinct individuals. Be sure to include at least one committee member who has sufficient expertise in the kind of methodology and analysis procedures you anticipate using. Finally, do not forget the important need for social support in the dissertation process. We suggest the inclusion of a committee member who can provide some emotional sustenance during inevitable periods of frustration.

Be mindful of typical committee procedures. Remember that faculty are inevitably busy people, so that you must provide sufficient lead time for them to make responses to drafts and inquiries. It is very reasonable to ask when a response might be forthcoming. Furthermore, you cannot assume that faculty will guard your proposal or dissertation drafts with the same vigilance that you would. Make copies of all documents under all circumstances, including backups of computer files. Our experience, exemplified by a student who recently lost all existing copies of her dissertation materials in a fire, suggests that backup copies should be stored in a different location. It is truly tragic whenever a manuscript or data are "lost" and there is no surviving record.

EMOTIONAL BLOCKS

We have discovered that technical supervision and consultation with graduate students is not the only kind of support instrumental in facilitating successful completion of the dissertation. The task itself also has a way of stimulating emotional issues that can, if overlooked, stymie the process. It is not unusual for the dissertation process to elicit all kinds of blows to self-esteem. Along the way it is quite common to feel that you will never reach the end of the trail. Some students don't know when to give up on a dead-end idea and switch horses to another topic, while other students fail to stay on a horse long enough to negotiate the necessary pitfalls along the road. It is not unusual to question a choice of topic or method and to torture oneself about it. If you are overly compulsive, you will inevitably think that you have left something out and the dissertation will never feel finished. Students need to maintain a perspective that allows them to know that frustration is predictable and that this too will end. One way of maintaining this perspective is to do the dissertation in small steps by selecting definable targets along the way and by calling on others for emotional support when feelings of failure loom large.

The challenge of completing an acceptable dissertation may also invoke deeply felt beliefs about incompetence and the inability to master this task. In our experience the dissertation process more often than not stirs up a student's most basic behavioral patterns and emotional vulnerabilities. Here is a sample of the kinds of issues that have been presented by students we know:

- The belief that completing the dissertation and obtaining the doctoral degree will be a sign of disloyalty to parents and family members who never came nearly so far in their own educational pursuits.
- The belief that completing the dissertation and obtaining the doctoral degree will bring a greater sense of responsibility and promise of future achievements that seem scary and unattainable.
- The belief that completing the dissertation and obtaining the doctoral degree will cost a marriage or relationship due to the threat of living with a "doctor," especially if one is a woman.
- The belief that the intelligence it takes to complete a dissertation is way beyond my capacities.

- The belief that I am an imposter, only "pretending" to be capable of completing a dissertation.
- The belief that there is no end in sight, that the dissertation will never be accepted as complete.
- The belief that I will have to give up my ideals and sell my soul to complete the dissertation.

This list of beliefs may seem trivial or inappropriate for students at the doctoral level of graduate education. On the contrary, we are convinced that these feelings and attitudes are more common than we usually admit and that they frequently stand in the way of progress on the dissertation. In our program we use supervision groups that encourage students to share not only their substantive research ideas with one another and with faculty, but also their fears and doubts about themselves in the process. We have found that sensitive exploration of these blocks can often forward the process as much as technical support. We have also been gratified to discover that students can generally identify and access significant coping skills that they may never have realized they possessed.

TASK BLOCKS

Writing a dissertation is a time-consuming, fundamentally lonely act that generally takes in the neighborhood of two years from start to finish. No matter how secure your social support system, you will need to generate great persistence to complete it. Some compulsivity helps, but so does preparatory organization of space and time.

A block that is part emotional and part cognitive is the inability to manage time. It should come as no surprise that our universities are full of A.B.D.s, that is, students who have satisfactorily completed all requirements for the doctoral degree other than the dissertation. One of the most common reasons for this state of affairs is the inability to deal with time constraints adequately. To be sure, the dissertation is the singular most time consuming graduate requirement. Because the completion of courses generally relies upon the structure of a graduate program, the indeterminate freedom of the dissertation may be a cause for alarm and paralysis. Here are some tips for arranging your life to conform to the task of completing the dissertation:

1. Give yourself privacy and quiet. Arrange a space or area of your house or office that is identified with studying and only studying. This is particularly important in the dissertation process. Make this space sacred so that you engage in other tasks, such as writing bills and talking on the telephone, in other areas. This is a straightforward application of the behavioral principle of stimulus control.

2. Taken as a whole, a dissertation can seem like a forbidding and overwhelming challenge. Use the principle of successive approximations to divide it into manageable slices. Tackle the dissertation one step at a time—the review of the literature, the research question and statement of the problem, the method, the results, and the discussion.

3. Get your thoughts on paper. Don't allow yourself to obsess and mull over ideas too long without putting those ideas down in type. Seeing words on a page or on a computer screen has a way of generating momentum. Don't worry at the outset if your words aren't polished. The important thing is to develop a pattern of producing some output on a regular basis.

4. Talk your ideas over with others. Some people, especially extroverted individuals, seem to do their best thinking through discussing ideas with others. Other people prefer to get away by themselves and listen to their own inner voice. In either case, discussing your ideas with friends and colleagues can help you view your work from a fresh perspective and keep you motivated.

5. Establish a regular weekly schedule that allows for several hours of concentrated dissertation time. Many of our students recommend reserving some time each day for the dissertation. Your own schedule will, of course, be influenced by your other commitments, but the important thing is the structure and the regularity. A firm schedule will help guide you through the inevitable stages when ideas are not forthcoming, when obstacles arise, or when temptations lure you to greener pastures.

6. Recognize that even the most productive plowhorse needs a break now and then. Give yourself some time off for enjoyable distractions and do so in a way that reinforces progress. If you find yourself violating your schedule and taking a brief vacation from your dissertation, be gentle and forgiving.

Inevitably, many ordinary life activities will be put on hold during the dissertation. It is crucial to be sensitive to family members because you will no doubt have to negotiate time off from normal responsibilities and contact with them. In our experience, when students graduate with their doctoral degrees, they are most appreciative of the unrequited support and tolerance of their family members in dealing with the impact of the dissertation. Moreover, a negative, impatient spouse can sabotage your progress. One way of encouraging ongoing support is to keep one's partner fully informed about the status and content of the dissertation. Otherwise, it is too easy to feel left out and neglected when a significant other is engaged in a scholarly project that may seem arcane, trivial, or simply interminable.

GETTING ORGANIZED: A CASE STUDY

One of the major tasks of completing a dissertation is maintaining control of the sheer magnitude of the project. You may be testing multiple hypotheses, with different instruments using numerous statistical analyses. In this section we report on how one student managed the project. This student, Helen Barrett, Ph.D., lives in Alaska and was unable to meet with her committee on a regular basis. Therefore, it was extremely important for her to develop clear and informative presentations of research design and hypothesis testing procedures. Barrett was interested in the relationship between learning style, adult self-directed learning, and personal computer competency. Her dissertation (Barrett, 1990) involved the testing of 10 hypotheses and a number of subsidiary questions. Data collection required questionnaire and interview strategies and data analysis included both quantitative and qualitative methods. In order to make her plans clear to both her committee and herself Barrett developed two tables, which are reproduced in their entirety here. The first, "Hypotheses, Instruments and Statistical Analysis," is presented in Table 8.1.

Note that the hypotheses are included in their entirety in the left-hand column and form the rows of the table. Barrett utilized four instruments plus personal interviews to obtain her data. These instruments consisted of a Questionnaire that Barrett designed to assess specific aspects of computer use, a Personal Computer Competency Inventory (PCCI), the Kolb Learning Style Inventory (LSI),

Table 8.1 Hypotheses, Instruments, and Statistical Analysis

Hypothesis	GQ	PCCI	LSI	SDLR	Variables	Stat Test
H1.1: Competent computer users spend more than 70% of the time learning their computers using self-directed learning strategies.	#17				IND = Level of PCC DEP = % Time SDL	Mean & St. Dev.
H1.2: Competent computer users will have a higher level of self-directed learning readiness than beginning computer users.				Total Score	IND = Level of PCC DEP = SDLRS Score	ANOVA
H1.3: Computer users with intrinsic motivation to learn how to use a personal computer have a higher relative level of personal computer competency than those with extrinsic motivation to learn.	#3 & 4	Total Score			IND = Source of Motivation DEP = PCCI Score	ANOVA & Chi-Square
H1.4: Computer users with a foundation for learning will have a higher level of personal computer competence	#9, 5, 6, 10, 31, 30, 15, 16, 21	Total Score			IND = Prior Experience, Sources of Assistance, Hours spent, typing speed, user group, PC ownership DEP = PCCI Score	ANOVA & Chi-Square
H2.1: Computer users with an active learning style will have a higher relative level of personal computer competence than those with a reflective learning style.		Total Score	AE-RO		IND = Learning Style DEP = PCCI Score	ANOVA
H2.2: Computer users with an abstract learning style will have a higher relative level of personal computer competence than those with a concrete learning style.		Total Score	AC-CE		IND = Learning Style DEP = PCCI Score	ANOVA
Subsidiary Question: What is the relationship between learning style and readiness for self-directed learning?			Four Styles	Total Score	IND = Learning Style DEP = SDLRS Score	ANOVA
H3.1: Computer users with a concrete learning style preference will favor the Graphical User Interface.	#33		AC-CE		IND = Learning Style DEP = Interface Preference	Chi-Square
H3.2: Computer users with an abstract learning style preference will favor the text-based user interface.	#33		AC-CE		IND = Learning Style DEP = Interface Preference	Chi-Square
H3.3: Competent users of graphical user interface computers will use more types of applications than competent users of text-based systems.	#8	# Apps			IND = Level Expertise DEP = # of Applications	2-Way ANOVA
H3.4: The type of computer learned has a greater impact on learning strategies than the learners' preferred learning style.	#10, 18, 14	Total Score	AC-CE AE-RO		IND = Learning Style IND = Type of Interface DEP = Strategies	ANOVA Chi-Square

SOURCE: From Barrett (1990). Reprinted with permission.
NOTE: Legend.
GQ = General Questionnaire; LSI = Learning Styles Inventory; SDLR = Self-Directed Learning Readiness; IND = Independent Variable; DEP = Dependent Variable; PCCI = Personal Computer Competency Inventory.

the Self-Directed Learning Readiness Scale (SDLRS), and personal interviews. Each of these is listed in columns following the hypotheses. By examining the cells formed by crossing the hypothesis with the instruments one can determine which instruments will be used to examine which hypotheses. The pound sign (#) is used to indicate that the total score on an instrument was used. If particular items, subscales, or factor scores derived from an instrument are used, these are indicated in the cells. Following the instruments is a column of variables, which lists the independent and dependent variable for each hypothesis. In the last column, Barrett presents the type of statistical analysis that will be used to examine each hypothesis. By examining this table one can determine exactly how Barrett is proposing to test each hypothesis in her research. This was not all that Barrett did to make things simple for her committee. She also developed an "Overview of Research Design," which is presented as Table 8.2.

In Table 8.2 the columns are formed by the concepts of her study (learner characteristics, computer competency, learning style, self-directed learning, and learning strategies). For each major concept Barrett has provided the instrument to be used, the type of data gathered, the type of scores produced, and the hypotheses addressed. The remaining space was used to present her proposal for a final synthesis and summary of the findings.

We have not polished these tables to make them acceptable for presentation in this book, they are presented exactly as Barrett constructed them. These tables allow Barrett, committee members, statistical consultants, and anyone else with an interest in this research to obtain immediately a picture of the study in question. We offer this example as a model for use in making your own research clear to yourself and to others.

COLLECTING AND ANALYZING DATA: DEPENDING UPON OTHERS

It is one thing to control your own behavior and quite something else to manage the behavior of others. There are at least two occasions when helpers or consultants may predictably become involved in the dissertation. One is in setting up the study and collecting the data; the other is in analyzing the data. Many dissertations require the cooperation of agencies and institutions, particularly to access pools of available and suitable subjects. Sometimes it is possible to

Table 8.2 Overview of Research Design

Adult Self-Directed Learning, Personal Computer Competency and Learning Style: Models for More Effective Learning

Components of Study

	Learner Characteristics	Personal Computer Competency	Learning Style	Self-Directed Learning Readiness	Learning Strategies
Instrument	General Questionnaire	PCCI Bersch/Barrett Personal Computer Competency Inventory	LSI Kolb Learning Style Instrument	SDLRS Self-Directed Learning Readiness Scale	Optional Additional Questions
Type of Data Gathered	Quantitative Demographic Data	Quantitative (Single response on list of 60 competencies)	Quantitative (12 questions with forced responses to 4 words/phrases	Quantitative (58 Likert Scale responses)	Qualitative Responses to open-ended questions
Type of Scores Produced	Single item indicators	Total Score plus ten clusters of computer applications skills	Two polarity scores (AE-RO and AC-CE) plus one of four Learning Styles	Total Score plus eight Self-Directed Learning Factors	Analysis of responses by question

Final Synthesis and Summary of Findings:

   1. Report findings related to hypotheses

   2. List of questions found to warrant further study

   3. Graphic model of learning process

   4. Suggested methods for "learning how to learn" personal computers

SOURCE: From Barrett (1990). Reprinted with permission.

graft a dissertation onto an ongoing research project of greater scope and magnitude. There is a lot to be said for this strategy. Much of the best research in any field is collaborative and involves a team of professionals coming together to complete a set of studies. If someone is currently engaged in a large research project, particularly one with grant funding and institutional support, that can be a great advantage. Captive subjects are available and it is often possible to add some additional measures or interventions to those that already constitute the focus of the study. If you choose and have the opportunity to go this route, there are a number of considerations to keep in mind:

1. Remember that a doctoral dissertation must be your own project, both in concept and in design, and that you need to retain ownership over it. This means that the data must be available to you to analyze as you see fit and that you must be free to describe whatever conclusions you reach, regardless of anyone's special interest or investment in the project as a whole. Do not rely on vague statements made in passing, particularly by those not in a position to guarantee you the use of a data set. Make your needs explicit and elicit promises regarding your involvement in a project and your use of the data. You also need to have the freedom to be able to publish the results in your own name.

2. Sometimes the scheduling of someone else's study may not conform to your own needs. We have found that students who collect dissertation or thesis data prior to having a completed, approved proposal do so at considerable risk. Method and procedures need to be in place and agreed upon prior to the start of data collection. This may be difficult if you are joining a larger study. It can also be tricky if your need for collecting data is governed by external considerations, such as the availability of school children at the beginning of the academic year or the established starting date of a program or group that you need to evaluate. The antidote to this problem is to plan ahead and assume that it will take longer to establish procedures than you imagine. Some very good research studies capitalize on the occurrence of unanticipated events that are ripe for data collection (e.g., a political revolution or ecological disaster), but they rarely result in doctoral dissertations.

3. It should go without saying that you and your committee are the final arbiters of the research questions and procedures of your study. It is not unusual for other people's large-scale projects to use measures or procedures that do not exactly measure what you intend to measure. Be certain that you have the freedom to make methodological changes that are critical to insuring the quality of your study. If you determine, for example, that the only measure of weight loss available to you is not a sufficient indicator of fitness, the setting for your proposed study may not be right.

A different kind of issue concerns the employment of peers to collect or code data. Many students have had the experience of serving in this role as research assistants. However, when graduate students use research assistants, they may not hold the same authority

over them as professors. In our experience, raters and other assistants often quit or do not reliably follow through on their commitments. It pays to be careful and conscientious in hiring assistants and
have backup strategies available if plans go awry. It is also important
to thoroughly train and supervise assistants at every step of the
process. What seems obvious to you, being totally immersed in your
study, may not be so obvious to someone else. A frequent problem
is obtaining low interrater reliability on coding data because the
raters have not been sufficiently trained.

DISSERTATION ORALS

The tradition of the final oral defense of the doctoral dissertation
is long-standing and likely to engender some anxiety in most doctoral students. The defense ranges from a congenial ritual in which
the student publicly presents his or her findings to an assemblage of
receptive "colleagues," to a more excruciating examination of the
quality of the dissertation and grilling of the candidate by an unsym-
pathetic faculty committee. In our view, no student should be al-
lowed to schedule a final dissertation oral defense if the dissertation
is not regarded as complete by the committee. Consequently, part of
the function of the defense is a formal "coming out" of the student
into the community of scholars, a celebration of the completion of a
major scholarly achievement, and a symbolic rite of passage to the
awarding of the doctorate. In the best of cases, the oral defense is an
opportunity to think about and articulate the implications of your
study to your own discipline and to be challenged by your committee
to claim your right to sit among them as an acknowledged expert in
your field of study.

To make the experience a positive one, there are a number of
reasonable preparations you can take. Certainly being fully familiar
with your study is crucial. It is likely that by the time of the oral
defense you will be a leading authority on your particular topic. The
more familiar you are with the details of your study, including the
relevant literature in the area, the more you will appear as the expert.
The role that the committee can rightly play is to provide some new
lenses through which to view your work because it is likely that by
this time you have stood so close to your own study that it may be
difficult to gain perspective and appreciate it from other vantage
points.

In the best of circumstances your committee will be aligned with your own goals of presenting your study as a colleague-to-be. Sometimes, unfortunately, the orals become an opportunity for faculty to build up their own egos at your expense. One recommendation for meeting this challenge is to take control of the situation as much as possible and move out of the victim position. One student we know scouted the site of his orals beforehand, rearranged the furniture in the room according to his preferences, and then greeted his committee personally as they entered the room.

Typically, students are asked to spend anywhere from 10 to 45 minutes providing an overview of their study at the outset of the orals. Think carefully about this task beforehand. Try to boil your presentation down to the essentials so that you do not overwhelm your audience with minutiae. Audiovisuals can help organize and illustrate a presentation, and slides and overheads are particularly effective ways of supporting a talk. Do not plan to chew up your allotted time with a long, drawn-out oral presentation in the hope that there will be no time for questions. Your committee is too smart for that and will assume that you are insufficiently knowledgeable for meaningful discussion of your work.

The presentation of the summary of the study is followed by questions and comments from the various committee members. On the basis of these comments, which can be benign or intimidating, the committee will determine their recommendations. In the best of circumstances, these rounds of questions can generate lively and enjoyable discussion about the study and the topic that will further establish your credibility as a professional. The more you can frame the final oral defense of the dissertation as an opportunity to present your research publicly, the better the experience is apt to be. The more you take a proactive, nondefensive position, the less likely it is for your committee to humiliate you. Count on being asked a few questions you will not be able to answer. That does not mean the end of the world. It may even be wise to "save something for the committee" so that they can make an acknowledged contribution to the completion of the project.

The most likely outcome of any dissertation orals is a pass with the request for minor revisions. Minor revisions are changes to the dissertation that do not impugn the central thesis, perhaps some additions to the bibliography, some further analyses, some elaborated discussion. Major changes are more substantive alterations to theory and method and thus more troublesome. The general antidote to the request for major changes is to keep your committee fully informed about the dissertation throughout the process by inviting them to read every chapter as it comes off the press. The more you request feedback during the two years or so of dissertation work, the less likely that a committee member will sabotage the entire dissertation at the orals stage. Be wary of the committee member who remains on the fringe of your project and does not have time to read your dissertation. This is a likely person to ask questions about statistics, because asking these sorts of questions does not require knowledge of your field or even the content of your dissertation. Have a good understanding of why you used each statistic for each analysis. Then you will be prepared for questions such as, "Well, Mr. Jones, why did you use an analysis of variance to assess hypothesis three?"

There tends to be a significant letdown for students at the conclusion of successfully defending their dissertations. Often this emotional letdown includes not wanting to see the dissertation ever again. We encourage you to respond to the request for changes as soon as possible. Otherwise, completion of the dissertation may drag on interminably. Moreover, we have found that if a student does not make a concerted effort to publish the results of the findings shortly after the orals, in either book or journal article form, it is unlikely that it will ever happen. Some departments attempt to counteract the resistance to publishing quality dissertations by accepting finished dissertations in publication form, perhaps including a broader review of the literature and discussion as appendices. In any case, for all those graduate students who have precipitously forgotten their dissertations on the way home from the orals, there are others who have launched their careers by distilling the dissertation into one or more promising publications.

The doctoral dissertation is apt to be the singular most ambitious research project of most social scientists' careers. As such, it not only has the potential for providing an entrée into a field of professional practice and scholarship, but it serves as an ongoing source of self-esteem and scholarship. It is a transformative experience. Paradoxically, whereas most students look back upon their dissertation experience as gruelling, overwhelming, and oftentimes aversive, students also evaluate the experience as confirming, life-changing, and an important transition into the world of the professional scholar.

9 ✔

Writing

Jody Veroff

Knowing how to express ideas in written form is an essential skill for the researcher. From the beginning of any research project to its final report, most researchers will spend more time writing about their ideas, their understandings of previous theory and research, and their own procedures, findings, and conclusions than they will spend actually conducting experiments or performing statistical analyses. It is easy to ignore how much of "science" depends on the communication of ideas in written form. It is also easy to ignore how much the ability to write clear and interesting prose contributes to the success of any research you may undertake. Well-written proposals are more likely to be:

- Received positively by funding agencies or dissertation committees
- Accepted for publication in professional journals
- Understood and appreciated by the audiences they reach

Thus the ultimate impact of any research you undertake is likely to be much enhanced if you can write well about your work.

You can learn a good deal about "how to write a research report" by referring to books and articles whose explicit focus is on this topic. I have listed some references in the bibliography at the end of this chapter. These will teach you conventional approaches to organizing and formatting your work and will help you mirror the characteristic logic and development of research writing. You can also study the writing style and organization of articles in professional journals that publish research reports in areas related to your research topic. Modeling these will probably guarantee that your report complies sufficiently with that journal's requirements to be acceptable. Unfortunately, many models available in professional journals are masterpieces of indirection, obfuscation, and sheer boredom. Some existing models support the suspicion that the writer has specifically aimed to make the report impossible for the average reader to understand, intending to speak only to an elite audience whose existing understanding of the topic is complete enough to interpret and translate what has been written. Indeed, this approach to writing about research is so prevalent that you might give it the label "journalese." If you use such writing as your model, you may persuade some readers that your work is important and profound since they cannot understand anything you have written, but you will also lose the opportunity to inform and communicate with a readership that is not already in the inner circle.

At one time or another most of us have been deeply affected by a scientific article because it helped us understand something we previously could not understand or because it engaged our own thinking and emotions in a way that stimulated our thought about the topic. If you wish your writing to affect readers in this way, it is important to pay attention to your writing style and to learn to express your ideas with clarity, with energy, perhaps even with grace. You will need to learn how to:

- Write what you mean
- Choose words and ways of putting them together that convey your understandings directly
- Avoid scientific jargon and stylistic "journalese"
- Identify with your potential readers and try to imagine their process of understanding what you have written

Learning how to write this way seems to me to be no different than learning how to write for any other purpose. Because, for many of us, something about both the realities and myths of "scientific writing" turns our minds to stone or slush and makes us feel awkward, stupid, and convoluted in our very thinking process, it may be easier to learn how to improve our writing in general than to begin with the specific demands of research writing.

PAST EXPERIENCES WITH WRITING

One way to demystify the process of writing is to retrace your history as "a writer." Remembering your own experiences may help you understand current pleasures you have as a writer as well as negative feelings and writing problems. Although the joys and sorrows of your own past experiences with writing are undoubtedly unique, there are commonalities in human development and similarities in educational structures that typically influence the way most of us learn to write. A brief review of these may help you retrieve some of your own past experiences and may help you understand current feelings and difficulties you may have with writing. Remembering and reappraising these experiences may also suggest ways to change your feelings and to take steps to remedy your difficulties.

LEARNING TO DISTANCE YOURSELF
FROM WRITING

Your writing career probably began at a tender age when you learned how to write your own name, a triumphant accomplishment even if the process was laborious and painful and the final product misshaped and awkward. Writing your name may not seem like "real writing" because it has only to do with learning how to shape letters, but it is the beginning of being able to express yourself on paper, the beginning stage of a new way to communicate with others about your thoughts and feelings. Unfortunately, subsequent education can encourage you to put more and more distance between your writing and your self, so that you learn not to value your own voice and may even conclude that your voice is an inappropriate presence in writing. You may learn to ignore personal ownership of writing or any real connection between what you write and who you are or what you think or feel.

This distancing of the self from writing is perhaps inevitable, given the predictable lag between conceptual abilities and the skills required to render thoughts on paper. Stubby little fingers often cannot keep up with the complex ideas that young children may want to express; the spoken vocabularies they command are usually far more extensive and sophisticated than the reading or writing vocabularies they master in the first few years of school. Learning to write "Run, run, run" or "See Betty catch the ball" may be a significant achievement for a first-grade child, but one that is essentially mechanical and that has little connection with his own thoughts or the way he talks about his world.

Distancing writing from the self may also be a consequence of the typical educational priorities that tend to focus on the development of essential skills such as penmanship, spelling, and grammar. It can be argued that children need to master these skills before they can use writing to express ideas, but there is considerable risk that the disconnection between such skill-learning and the child's ongoing experience will teach him or her that writing does not have much to do with himself or herself and the things he or she might like to say on paper. Even when writing skills are essentially in place, later school experience may continue to reinforce a separation between the child's own thoughts and feelings and the process of writing. Writing projects are likely to be geared toward teaching the child how to use libraries and reference materials and requiring him or her to demonstrate the facts he or she has learned from his or her "research."

In my schooling years, students had little choice about topics for writing projects; when your geography class was studying the New England region, you could write about "The Principal Products of Lowell, Massachusetts" or a similar topic from a limited list. Although I hope and think that children currently have more choice in the topics they must write about, public libraries are still full of young children straining their eyes over encyclopedias, keeping their place with one hand while they write down information with the other. It is easy to imagine that they are writing, just as I did, papers on "The Honey Bee" or "The Mountains of Peru" or "Diphtheria," without much interest in their topic and without much inclination to go beyond recording the information provided in the encyclopedia.

LEARNING TO THINK OF WRITING
AS A BORING ACTIVITY

Using writing projects to augment standard classroom learning or to assess whether children have mastered the skills required to collect information about a topic is a reasonable way to teach children important academic skills. A regrettable conclusion that children may draw, however, is that the purpose of writing is to write down someone else's information about a subject that is not very interesting. Part of their learning may be that writing is a tedious and unrewarding activity to be put off as long as possible. The experience of understanding more about a topic by writing about it and the pleasure of writing about something of personal interest and importance can be rare and unusual for the average child going through school. It is not surprising then that so many of us grow up to view writing as burdensome.

LEARNING TO FEEL INADEQUATE AS A WRITER

In the later years of grade school and on through high school and college, teachers become increasingly evaluative of their students' writing and are particularly alert to errors in grammar, punctuation, and spelling, sometimes to the exclusion of attention to the content or the way ideas have been developed. Most of us can remember the sinking sensation provoked when writing assignments were returned, covered with red ink and graphically showing how many errors we had made on every page. Although we searched in vain for any evidence that the teacher liked what we said or the way we said it, we found instead that the comments in the margins informed us only of where we had been unclear, illogical, or awkward. Whatever pleasure or excitement we might have felt about the original writing assignment was usually diluted and tarnished. Some of us may remember feeling so stupid and unskilled that we began to be afraid to write papers at all. Although students with some "natural" gift for writing well and those with more compassionate teachers may escape such aversive experiences, many people respond to less affirming school experiences by learning to be afraid to write. As teachers, especially at the college level, become more and more concerned about the inability of many students to write at even a minimally acceptable level, there is every reason to expect that they will redouble their efforts to point out error and will be less and less inclined to notice or reward the ideas the student has expressed.

This review of common educational experiences around writing has focused on those that foster the following beliefs:

- It is not quite appropriate to write about your own ideas.
- Writing is primarily a boring rehash of other people's ideas.
- What has been written will be vigilantly read by evaluators to see how many mistakes they can notice.

For those of us whose experience was primarily tilted in this way, it is surprising that we do not give up on writing altogether once we have finished high school or college. And, it is not surprising if we learned to be afraid to write or to have difficulty in getting ourselves to sit down and write, or to believe we are not good writers. Yet most of us continue to write. We write down lists of things to do today, we write directions to the baby sitter or the plumber, we write business letters, letters of complaint, letters of explanation, letters of sympathy and condolence, and occasional letters of thank you. Although the writing of friendly letters is mourned by some as a dying art, some of us still write to our mothers or our children or our friends who live in distant places. If our work requires it, we write progress reports and project proposals and memos and instructions, all without crippling anxiety or resistance. The old aversive feelings about writing emerge most dramatically when we must write something that someone else will receive and evaluate as "serious" writing. Writing about theory or research may provoke the most intense concern; not only are there conventions and myths about conventions for this kind of writing that limit our freedom of expression, but also writing about more abstract topics is generally difficult, especially when we do not fully understand the ideas. Although the very process of struggling to write about ideas is often clarifying and can promote deeper comprehension, it is tempting to circumvent this struggle by stringing words and phrases and clauses together in a way that is sufficiently obscure so that no one will be able to detect the line of thought anyway.

If you are burdened with anxiety about your writing or by a perpetual reluctance to begin to write or by a conviction that the demands of writing well require a gift that you do not have, do not despair. If you can think and if you can speak about what you think, there is little likelihood that you cannot learn to write. You are even a good candidate for learning to enjoy writing. The major obstacles that you need to overcome are: (a) *fear*, engendered by past unpleasant experiences associated with writing; (b) *boredom*, resulting from not caring enough about what you are writing about; (c) *perfectionism*, that makes you labor too hard over each word you use or worry too much about evaluation or try to render in full detail everything that has ever been said about your topic; (d) *disenfranchisement* from your own voice and your own ideas, that makes you feel unentitled to express your ideas in a form that others can examine and evaluate; (e) *impatience*, that allows you to imagine that writing should be quick and easy, an activity that doesn't require the time and effort ordinarily necessary to learn to do anything well; (f) *excessive pride* that makes you believe that your public expressions should be wonderful, thus making you unwilling to reveal that sometimes they are not. Additional obstacles may reside in difficulties with spelling, grammar, and sentence structure, but these obstacles can usually be overcome by learning the rules of the grammatical structure of English, by enlisting an editor or proofreader, by employing word processing programs designed to pick up such errors, or by using a dictionary and a guide to common grammar and spelling errors.

OVERCOMING OBSTACLES

Overcoming the obstacles created by negative experiences and unrealistic expectations may sound quite formidable, something that might require a substantial therapeutic intervention to achieve. It is not always easy to lay anxiety to rest, or to give up perfectionism or concern about evaluation. Reflections of successful writers on their work suggest that these problems continue to haunt even the best of writers, many of whom suffer from writer's block for extended periods of time and often struggle on a daily basis to keep themselves writing. Most emphasize the importance of regular writing and describe strategies they employ to make sure they do this. There is a common recognition that it is often easier not to begin to write, just as it might be easier not to do the dishes or go jogging or practice the piano. But all skills require regular practice and most of us are accustomed to imposing sufficient discipline in our lives to attend to the things we consider important. Writers often schedule blocks of time when they will write each day or set goals for the number of pages they will complete. They take their work as writers seriously enough to organize their lives so that their writing time is at least as sacred as the time they allot to other activities. If you want to learn to write, it is essential to make writing a regular and routine activity that is at least as important to you as brushing your teeth or reading the newspaper. There will be no better way to increase your skill and your comfort.

GETTING STARTED

MAKING LISTS

It is all very well to urge you to write frequently and regularly, but resolving to do so may not necessarily protect you from the depressing circumstance of staring at a pristine yellow legal pad or a blank computer terminal, wondering how in the world to begin. Even if there is a writing project that you urgently need to complete, you may find yourself quite literally at a loss for words. Sometimes it helps to fall back on the kinds of writing most of us do every day. You might, for example, begin by making a list of ideas that seem important to address in your paper. List-making is a familiar and comfortable activity that does not have to be any more profound and meaningful than a shopping list or a list of things to do today. Yet, just as these prosaic lists help to organize your thoughts and priorities, a list of ideas that seem important can begin to organize the shape of the piece you want to write. A good list can be played with. You can put the items in order of importance, so that your list can remind you of what most needs to be included just as a list of things to do today reminds you of the priority of paying the electric bill before they turn off the lights. You can also organize a list by establishing which things should be first and last and somewhere in the middle, just as a list of errands might remind you to take the casserole out of the freezer first and buy the ice cream last. A list can help you take into account the way some of the ideas are related to others and need to be clustered together just as a useful shopping list groups lettuce, apples, and potatoes together separate from butter, eggs, and milk. Playing with your list of ideas in this way can give you a structure for your writing project that will allow you to get started and to know where you are going.

CLUSTERING

If the linearity of lists stultifies you and you have never been able to make an outline until you have written your piece, a different way of beginning may be more in tune with your thinking style. In her book *Writing the Natural Way*, Gabriele Rico (1983) describes a method she believes helps writers to access the natural structuring tendencies of the human brain. She calls this method "clustering." It begins with a free associative task that involves first writing your topic somewhere in the middle of a piece of paper and then writing words and phrases that come to mind around the central topic with no conscious attention to their spatial placement. As more and more apparently random associations are recorded, you can begin to draw lines between ideas that seem connected and otherwise begin to fill in the "map" of associated thoughts. Rico contends that at some point a structure emerges that will allow you to write a reasonably well-formed paragraph about your topic that links and organizes your ideas in a coherent form that represents your current understanding of your topic. I have used this exercise in writing workshops; it does seem to allow most participants to produce a coherent paragraph in a very short period of time. A few people in each group have found this method so liberating and helpful that they feel their approach to thinking and writing has been virtually transformed. If you are stuck and cannot get yourself to begin to write, you will risk little by trying this method and you may be lucky and discover that it is uniquely compatible with your way of thinking.

WRITING A LETTER TO A FRIEND

Another way to trick yourself into beginning is to pretend you are writing to a friend to tell her about your topic and what you have learned about it. Suppose you are interested in exploring whether or not men and women go through different processes in deciding to run for political office. If you were writing about this interest to a friend, you would probably want to tell her why you were interested in this topic, why you think it is important, what hunches you have about differences that might exist. Trying to imagine what you would need to tell her to help her understand all of this may help you begin to write and begin to organize your thoughts about the topic without feeling as intimidated as you might if you were imagining your reader to be your dissertation chair or the review committee of a funding agency. Because you may know already what your friend thinks and knows about gender differences or running for political office, you will be able to imagine how she might receive and react to what you have written and foresee some of the arguments you may have to present to persuade her that this is an important issue to study. Beginning as if you were writing to a friend will highlight the communicative aspect of writing and remind you of the importance of your self in the communicative relationship that is created by writing. It will encourage you to write about your ideas in simple, direct and nontechnical language. And it may allow you to make connection with why you care about your topic. If your "letter to a friend" instead adds fear that your topic is so boring that no one could possibly want to read about it, perhaps the exercise will help you decide to find a better topic.

JOURNALISTIC DEVICES

Introductory classes in journalism suggest another trick that may help you get started. Fledgling reporters are instructed to begin every news story with a first paragraph that tells the reader *Who? What? Why? When?* and *Where?* (An additional query—*How?*—is a useful addition in writing about research). Reporters learn to put this essential, bare bones information in the lead paragraph so that a coherent account of the news will remain even if space limitations require cutting the remainder of their story. This journalistic device can be usefully employed to get started on any writing project even when you have no reason to fear that your audience will not read beyond your first paragraph. This format may help you get started because it describes a small and delimited task that will help organize your writing and remind you to include the information necessary to tell your reader what your article will be about. It can often become the introductory paragraph of your paper. If you wish, for example, to write about the problem of inner-city violence in adolescents, a good introduction might be:

> Escalating violence among inner-city adolescents (what?) is becoming a major social problem that exacts an enormous toll in young lives and crime control costs. Understanding the causes of this escalation is, thus, an imperative research agenda. (why?) This study will survey a sample of 15-19 year old adolescents (who?) attending school in Detroit, Michigan (where?) in the fall of 1992 (when), using attitude questionnaires (how?) to identify their perceptions of the causes of violence in the schools.

The relatively simple task of answering the journalistic questions results in an introduction that states the purpose and approach of the study clearly and directly and prepares the reader for the elaborations that will follow. Your reader can then make a decision about whether or not he or she is sufficiently interested in your topic and your approach to read further.

WRITING STORIES

If you are a person who likes to tell stories, you might find it useful to write about your topic in story form. The story of how you came to be interested in your topic might be a natural way to begin. Or you might tell the story of how you learned more about your topic. Most of us learned the basic structure of a story when we were very young and know by heart the convention that begins with "once upon a time" and ends with "and they lived happily ever after." In between the beginning that sets the stage and the ending that brings things to a satisfying conclusion we know that characters must be introduced, some kind of problem must be posed that leads to some kind of action that allows for the "happy ending," with enough tension and suspense built in so that the reader cares to keep on reading. You may find it a bit odd to think of writing a research report as if it were a story, but some of the most engaging and interesting examples of scientific writing have qualities similar to a good detective story. The writer describes the "mystery," tells you how she developed her "clues" and how she went about collecting the evidence, and how she ruled out various "wrong" solutions on her way to discovering a convincing answer to the mystery. This device is especially useful in writing about research findings and theories in social science, where the phenomena under consideration are often complex and potential "causes" are both multiple and interactive. Researchers and theorists often begin with a relatively simple hypothesis such as, for example, that increased stress will lead to an increased rate of illness. But the plot soon thickens and researchers must begin to attend to other factors that influence this relationship, eventually constructing a "cast of characters" that play a role in how stress affects well-being. Writing the "story" that describes the hunches that have been followed up, the "red herrings" in the case, the new clues that emerge, the new evidence that must be collected would be an engrossing way to present the literature relevant to this topic that might in itself generate new insights.

Each of these devices for getting started provides a way to organize your thoughts and ideas that should allow you to put some words on your blank piece of paper or your empty computer terminal. You may also be able to see where the rest of your writing project will be going and the kind of structure it will have, because each of these devices creates a purpose for what you are writing:

- To order your ideas
- To recognize the connections between ideas
- To make sense of your ideas in ordinary language
- To persuade someone about your way of thinking
- To provide your reader with essential information
- To tell the story of the development of your ideas

If your writing does not initially seem to have a purpose beyond satisfying the requirements of an assignment, these devices may help you generate other purposes that will facilitate the writing process and make it more interesting.

TOPIC AND PASSION

If you have any choice at all about topics for your writing, choosing one that you care about and are interested in may be one of the most important things you can do to facilitate your writing. Although some advisors warn against choosing topics with high personal relevance on the grounds that your appropriate objectivity will be impaired, this danger is small compared to the problems that arise when you try to write about something entirely divorced from your personal experience, concern, or interest. The energy required to sustain effort, to endure frustration, to think creatively flows most readily from passion for your topic. This may be a passionate desire to find answers to puzzling questions or a passionate curiosity to learn as much as possible about a topic of interest or a passion to communicate to others the important things you have discovered and learned. Passion not only provides energy that will propel your writing project onward, but it also helps guarantee that you will interact with the materials you are writing about, testing the ideas and information of others against your own thoughts and ideas and experiences. Thus what you write will be both more integrative and more likely to generate new insights for yourself and for your readers as well. Your evident investment in your topic will almost inevitably make what you write interesting to others. The energy derived from your passion and interest will be evident in your writing and will make what you write exciting for anyone who reads it.

Sometimes even a randomly chosen topic can inspire interest and passion as you learn more about it. You can recognize this when you find yourself wondering about something you have learned or wanting to argue with it or becoming eager to pursue the topic in greater depth. These are exciting moments in intellectual development and I do not want to suggest that you should eliminate such possibilities in your search for a topic. Especially when you are writing to fulfill an assignment in a class, you may find it initially difficult to think about anything you care very much about. Doing some general reading relevant to the course content before you select a topic for a writing project, and paying special attention to ideas that stimulate questions or connections or curiosity, will be useful in identifying a topic sufficiently interesting to sustain your writing momentum.

Even when you care about your topic, you may not be able to generate the kind of passion I have been describing if you content yourself with recording what is known about the topic. Such writing often becomes a kind of laundry list of what others have discovered or said about the subject and just as often is both boring to write and boring to read. The "detective mode" is usually more effective in communicating the excitement you feel about your topic. By this I mean the organization of your writing around questions that you have sought to answer and the possible answers that have presented themselves. The difference between writing about a *topic* and writing about *questions* could be described as the difference between reviewing what is known about a topic and identifying the relevance of what is known to the questions at hand. Although both approaches will communicate essentially the same information, the detective mode engages the writer in interacting with available information and is likely to engage the reader to interact similarly. Whenever you find yourself wondering why something is the way it is or how it works or who might be affected or whether it always happens this way or instead depends on something else to set it off, you have more than likely identified a good topic for both research and writing. Your questions will make you care about finding answers and will make it easier for you to write a well-organized, interesting paper.

AUTHORSHIP AND VOICE

Much of what I have said about caring and passion is directly related to another important attribute of good writing that I will call "claiming your authorship." Excluding your self from your writing is a good way to make your writing boring to yourself and others. The unfortunate tendency to exclude oneself as knower, scholar, interpreter, discoverer in writing is often learned very early in ways alluded to earlier. Educators in their eagerness to educate often emphasize the need for children to demonstrate *what* they have learned in their writing in tests and papers in order to make sure that children have the requisite knowledge of literature, geography, history, science, and all of the other things they might not know if they were not taught. Less often do they encourage students to think about what they have learned, to share those thoughts, or to write about what they may know from experience or from sources other than standard textbooks and reference materials. It is easy for children to conclude that "received knowledge" (cf. Belenky, Clinchy, Goldberger, & Tarule, 1986) is more true, more valuable, and more rewarded than any other kind of knowing. Received knowledge, by definition, comes from the authority of others and when the measurement of a child's learning is her ability to recite the knowledge she has received, it is difficult for her to perceive herself as entitled to be the author of knowledge.

Scholarly writing about theory and research generally requires the writer to go beyond recording received knowledge, and authors of such writing have almost always thought about issues, reached conclusions on the basis of available evidence, and interacted with their information in order to organize and integrate it. Yet, many theorists and researchers persist in using a style that suggests that it is inappropriate for the writer to acknowledge his or her authorship or involvement with what he or she has written. Conventions of referring to the self in the third person, never using the word *I*, predominantly using the passive voice suggest that even a writer who is discussing his or her own discoveries or his or her own theories must pretend it was someone else who thought or discovered or concluded. Of course when a writer says, "It was discovered that . . ." or "it is reasonable to conclude that . . ." we all know that he or she means "I discovered this" and "I conclude that," but the language style suggests that the knowledge he or she is presenting was received from somewhere else and did not really involve himself or herself. The extent to which prevailing conventions encourage the writer to disown what he or she has written in this way was dramatically brought home to me when I recently re-read my doctoral dissertation, written in 1959. I discovered to my chagrin that I had not only disowned my authorship but also my gender by referring throughout this document to my ideas in the masculine third person. Although current emphasis on nonsexist language probably protects young women writing today from such absurd constructions, they were not uncommon in those days and they provide graphic examples of how this convention of "scientific writing" influences the relationship of the writer to his or her writing. This kind of depersonalization is motivated not only by a reluctance to claim authority, but apparently also by an attempt to demonstrate objectivity by underplaying the fact that there is a real and potentially fallible person who has written about his or her own ideas and conclusions.

It serves to reinforce the fears of many that they are not entitled to have ideas or to think about topics or to draw their own conclusions. Claiming authorship requires taking responsibility for what you write; although this may be intimidating it is also empowering.

Although stylistic rules may require you eventually to disembody yourself in your writing, there is no rule that says you can't begin by openly acknowledging that "I wondered about this, I think these ideas are unsupported by evidence, I surveyed the literature, I designed a study, I concluded that. . . ." To do so will make you very aware that you are the author of what you write, responsible for what you say, and entitled to communicate your own ideas and understandings. If you must remove the "I" from your writing to satisfy the demands of others, it will be easier to find ways to do this that do not deny your authorship if you have first written more personally. The most recent edition of the *Publication Manual of the American Psychological Association* (1983, p. 35) makes the following observation about the use of the first person: "inappropriately or illogically attributing action in the name of objectivity can be misleading. For example, writing 'The experimenter instructed the subjects' when 'the experimenter' refers to yourself is at best ambiguous and may even give the impression that you disavow your own study." Although many journals and advisors continue to insist on the disembodied voice, it is likely that this change in a major arbiter of style will eventually influence changes in the requirements imposed by journal editors.

Developing a "voice" as a writer depends on a strong sense of yourself as the possessor of knowledge and ideas who is entitled to speak about these to others. The voices of writers such as Hemingway, Proust, Twain, or Freud are easily recognized (and can be easily parodied) by readers familiar with their work. If you claim authorship in your writing and practice doing so, your voice will become distinctive in much the same way as your fingerprint is or your way of walking. In this sense, developing your voice not only lends authority to your writing but tends to make writing a more "natural" process in which ways of expressing ideas or constructing sentences flow more easily without requiring as much conscious and deliberate effort.

No one develops a writing voice overnight and the steps that might hasten the process are not easy to describe. It requires not only developing your sense of entitlement to have ideas and to write about them, but also attention to your own characteristic modes of expression. The kind of words you like to use, the rhythm of your "natural" writing, the way you use metaphor and images to convey your ideas, the very organization that seems most natural in structuring your thoughts are part of your voice. An exercise that may be useful in alerting you to elements of your voice involves writing about a randomly chosen topic for several minutes with the explicit goals of writing whatever comes to mind and not allowing yourself to stop writing. Such "free writing" unmediated by conscious attention to content or "proper" form can provide helpful insights about your natural style of expression on paper.

An entertaining way to further explore issues of voice involves writing about a given situation from several different perspectives. A particularly illuminating way to do this might be to review a description of a psychological experiment. In the characteristic mode of objective science, it will most likely be written from the perspective of a disembodied, anonymous third person who presumably is reporting the facts about the experiment. Try writing about the experiment from the perspective of one of the subjects of the experiment, usually referred to as (S). Then write about the experiment from the perspective of the experimenter, trying to imagine his or her thoughts and feelings as he or she conducted the experiment. Finally, write a description of the experiment from your own perspective as a reader. The differences among your resulting descriptions reflect different voices and can help liberate your own voice and at the same time may give you new insights about what really happened during the experiment and what interpretations you may want to draw from it.

CONCERN ABOUT AUDIENCE AND EVALUATION

I have spoken earlier of the importance of recognizing that writing is a form of communication that involves not only the writer but also the potential reader. It is important to write with some awareness of your potential readers so that you can foresee what they will need to know to understand your ideas. Imagining the needs and interpretive skills of your reader is a way to provide yourself with critical feedback necessary to make sure that your writing communicates what you want to say in the clearest possible fashion. Writing with this kind of awareness of your potential readers is also a good way to retain the kind of liveliness and energy that often characterizes conversation.

There is, however, another kind of awareness of your potential readers that can be a serious obstacle in writing. When you allow yourself to become preoccupied with how the readers of your work will evaluate what you have written, you are likely to stifle the flow of your writing, sometimes to the point of suffocation. If you try to guess what your reader expects or wants you to say, it will be difficult to feel free enough to say what you want to say in a way that honestly reflects your own thinking and ideas. If you focus on trying to impress your readers with how much you know or how elegantly you can write about what you know, you will have lost sight of the real purpose of your writing, which presumably had something to do with ideas you wanted to express. Such a focus on how your writing will be evaluated by its readers may be one cause of writer's block since it encourages you to strive for a "perfect" piece of writing. Since what someone else will see as perfect is almost impossible to anticipate, you have set yourself an impossible task. For the extreme perfectionist, no sentence put down on paper is quite good enough and no choice of words exactly captures the idea the writer has in mind. Whenever you find yourself stuck on the first paragraph of a writing project, writing and rewriting your introduction, it may be helpful to ask yourself whose expectations you are trying to meet. Turning off the "editor in your head" may provide you with enough freedom to begin and continue to write a first draft that will be a more useful basis for corrections and revisions than a page full of false starts.

I can personally attest to the writing problems caused by over-concern with an evaluative audience; in the process of writing this chapter I have struggled at length and to no particular advantage with both the things I have been saying and the way I have been saying them because it seems highly presumptuous to write about writing if I do not demonstrate in the way I write that I am a sufficient authority to advise other people. I know that all that I can do is to write what I believe to be true about the challenge of writing, the obstacles that may emerge, the strategies I have found useful to deal with these; however, my acute awareness that I have exposed myself to public evaluation of my ideas, my writing style, and my logic has continuously impeded my progress and interrupted the flow of my thinking and my writing. It is both consoling and sobering to realize that some part of my audience may actually be relieved to see that a person writing about writing sometimes fails to write clearly or gracefully, but this does not entirely relieve the inhibition caused by overconcern with my audience.

My experience suggests that it is sometimes very difficult to turn off "the editor in your head." The need to do so is signaled when you find yourself struggling for a long time to think of the best way to express an idea or when you realize that you have been working and reworking a passage endlessly without achieving any sense of progress. At such times, it may help to resort temporarily to one or another of the "getting started" strategies I described earlier. Sketching in a passage by listing key ideas that you will return to on another day may allow you to move on. Shifting the focus of your attention from an evaluative audience by pretending you are writing to a friend or are writing a story may reduce your anxiety sufficiently to quiet your concern about all of the potential editors out there. Another useful strategy is to conjure up an alternative audience who may benefit in some way if only they have a chance to learn what you know and think about your topic. These tricks will probably afford only partial relief for a severe case of "editor anxiety," but may get you through the worst stage of total paralysis. Goldberg (1991), in her engaging book about writing, *Writing Down the Bones,* suggests still another strategy that sounds promising. When "the editor is absolutely annoying," she suggests that you write out your most damning version of what the editor will say about your work in full and gory detail. She observes that "the more clearly you know the editor, the better you can ignore it" (p. 26).

REVISION

Despite the fact that I have urged you not to strive for perfection in your writing, I do want to stress the importance of re-reading and revising what you have written. It is unlikely that any one of us can execute a first draft of a writing project that:

Check
list

- Says exactly what we want to say
- Provides all the information our readers need to understand what we have written
- Does not contain awkward sentences or ungrammatical constructions
- Cannot be significantly improved upon reconsideration

Reading aloud what you have written is an excellent way to *hear* the awkward phrases and grammatical errors that inevitably creep into any piece of writing. Because once you have committed your ideas to paper they are apt to seem complete and logical, asking someone else to read what you have written may be a way to get help in identifying places where your development of ideas is confusing or insufficiently supported by evidence even though it seems to make sense to you. It is easy to leave out crucial steps in an argument; we count on readers to follow our thought processes even when these have not been fully stated and sometimes expect them to be able to read our minds. A friendly reader can help us see when we have expected our audience to know more than they do and to fill in gaps in our writing that they cannot possibly manage to do. At the other extreme, problems arise from beating an argument to death by repeating essentially the same point over and over in slightly different form. Someone coming fresh to the writing piece is almost always more sensitive than the author to problems of either omission or redundancy.

In the days before word processors, writing successive drafts of a paper was a time-consuming and laborious task and writers' wastebaskets overflowed with crumpled sheets of paper containing false starts and discarded passages. Each draft usually involved extensive retyping of the previous draft and only the most persistent and committed writers could discipline themselves to undertake the multiple drafts that might lead to a final version they found fully acceptable. Composing papers from the start on the word processor allows for continuous revision and for free writing of sections that may ultimately fit best many pages later (or that may be deleted with the touch of a key). This is an extraordinary boon to many writers, although I still occasionally hear of writers who save their word processors for typing their final drafts. If you prefer to revise a completed draft rather than changing things as you go, you may still want to experiment with the freedom afforded by word processors to write anything that comes into your mind and consign it to oblivion in the next second or to save ideas that are not yet fully developed but that may become important as your writing project develops.

My use of a word processor has made me much more sensitive to my writing problems and much more willing to work to correct them; I hope and believe that it has resulted in considerable gains in my writing fluency. Although everyone may not find this tool as invaluable as I have, I do recommend at least experimenting with it. The freedom first to detach from overconcern about what you are writing or how you write and afterwards to reconstruct and revise what you have written so readily is likely to make first drafts easier to write and at the same time to increase your willingness to subject your work to the kind of revision that is almost always necessary.

CONCLUSION

There are many steps between the beginning stages of getting started, choosing a topic, and developing passion and voice, and the final stages of revision and completion of the writing project. These will be shaped by your writing purpose, your topic, and your audience and cannot easily be addressed in a single chapter about writing. At the end of this chapter, I have included a number of references that discuss "how to write" from different perspectives and for different purposes. The following list of "tricks" that summarize what has gone before may also help you keep your momentum from the beginning of your efforts to their successful conclusion.

TWELVE TRICKS TO KEEP YOU GOING WHEN YOU WRITE

1. At least in your first draft, use the first person singular to keep you in touch with *your* ideas, *your* reactions, *your* beliefs, *your* understandings of what other people have written. Enjoy your voice as AUTHOR. Speak as straightforwardly as you can. Avoid the passive voice whenever possible. If the requirements for publication or whatever dictate some other form, you can always revise later on.

2. Write as flamboyantly as you like in your first draft to give voice to your passion. If you like adverbs and adjectives, use them generously.

3. If it makes you nervous to assert your own position, qualify it as often as possible in your first draft. Brave statements seem less dangerous with lots of phrases like "in my opinion," "I think," "it seems to me," as well as "probably," "not infrequently," "perhaps," "in some instances." Better to get your words on paper than to get hung up by anxiety about whether you have the right or sufficient knowledge or adequate proof to make strong statements.

4. In the beginning try to forget how your audience might evaluate what you write or how you write it. There will be plenty of time later on to worry about the feedback that editors, publishers, or faculty advisors will inevitably give you. In the beginning, worrying about pleasing evaluating audiences is apt to lead to obsessing about each word you write, and you will often end up trying to impress your evaluators with your erudition, intellect, or elegance of phrase. This wastes a lot of time and energy.

5. Try to write in short sentences, especially in your first draft, so that you don't get tangled up in long convoluted sentences that can obscure your meaning. Much writing time is wasted trying to straighten out grammatical absurdities that would never exist in the first place if you tried to put just one idea in one sentence.

6. Try to find your own comfortable writing style and way of developing ideas. Be respectful of your style. If it is easy and useful for you to outline your ideas and then develop the outline into an essay, do that. If you spend more time making an outline than it would take to write the whole piece, don't let anyone convince you that you should make an outline. If you like to write in the middle of the night, do it. If you need to write around and around your topic until you finally get to the center of it, do it.

7. Do not be afraid to use the writing of others as a model. This is not a fraudulent act, but rather one that acknowledges how much we can learn from master craftspeople. When you come across a piece of writing that seems especially clear, forceful, and enjoyable to read, pay attention to how that writer organizes and communicates ideas.

8. Introduce discipline into your writing task by committing yourself to spending a given number of hours (or minutes) writing or to producing a given amount of written text every day. If it is hard to do this, set your goals low and don't allow yourself to exceed them in the beginning. Set an alarm clock, if necessary, and even if you are in the midst of an interesting idea, stop when the alarm goes off. You will soon find yourself more and more frustrated by having to interrupt your work and more and more eager to extend your writing time just a few more minutes. It is safe to do this, but feel free to go back to your time limits if you find yourself staring at your paper or out the window very long. If you write only a few paragraphs a day, you will probably have six or seven pages to show for your effort at

the end of one week. This is much more encouraging to most of us than spending four or five hours a day with nothing but aimless jottings or a wastebasketful of crumpled paper at the end of each work session.

LATER ON, WHEN YOUR FIRST DRAFT IS FINISHED AND YOU ARE READY TO REVISE YOUR WORK:

9. Remove all the adverbs and adjectives you so joyously put in your first draft and restore only those that are absolutely necessary to your meaning. If you have been outrageously emotional or have put yourself far out on a limb with your assertions, weed out some of the color and make sure you can defend what you have said with evidence.

10. Eliminate all your qualifying statements and restore only those that are necessary to be honest and to retain your meaning. Now that you are at the end of your project, you will feel braver about what you have written and will not need so much to hide behind disclaimers.

11. If all your short sentences sound choppy and telegraphic, combine some of your sentences to make a better flow. But be careful when you do this. If you can't combine two sentences without making a ponderous and incomprehensible whole, leave your short sentences alone. It is preferable to suffer a little choppiness than to leave your reader perplexed about what you mean to say. The rhythm that results from varying the length of your sentences can contribute variety and momentum to your writing that will make it more exciting to read.

12. Don't accept any of the foregoing rules or any other rule of writing that can't be broken or doesn't work for you. To paraphrase Julia Child's immortal words about making bread, remember that you are the boss of your writing.

GENERAL REFERENCES

Beale, W. H. (1982). *Real writing*. Glenview, IL: Scott, Foresman.
Belenky, M., Clinchy, B., Goldberger, N., & Tarule, J. (1986). *Women's ways of knowing: The development of self, voice and mind*. New York: Basic Books.

Cox, S. (1981). *Indirections for those who want to write.* Boston: David Godine.
Goldberg, N. (1991). *Writing down the bones/Wild mind.* New York: Quality Paperback Book Club.
Graves, R., & Hodge, A. (1966). *The reader over your shoulder.* New York: Collier Books.
Hall, D. (1973). *Writing well.* Boston: Little, Brown.
Howard, V. A. (1986). *Thinking on paper.* New York: William Morrow.
Jacobi, E. (1976). *Writing at work: Do's, don'ts, and how-to's.* Rochelle Park, NJ: Hayden.
Rico, G. L. (1983). *Writing the natural way.* Los Angeles: J. P. Tarcher.
Zinsser, W. (1988). *Writing to learn.* New York: Harper & Row.
Zinsser, W. (1990). *On writing well* (4th ed.). New York: Harper Perennial.

RESEARCH REPORT REFERENCES

Ballou, S. V. (1970). *A model for theses and research papers.* Boston: Houghton Mifflin.
Campbell, W. G., & Ballou, S. V. (1977). *Form and style: Theses, reports, term papers* (5th ed.). Boston: Houghton Miflin.
Davis, G. B., & Parker, C. (1979). *Writing the doctoral dissertation.* Woodbury, NY: Barron's Educational Series.
Hilbish, F. M. (1952). *The research paper.* New York: Bookman Associates.
Madsen, D. (1983). *Successful dissertations and theses.* San Francisco: Jossey-Bass.
Modern Language Association. (1977). *MLA handbook for writers of research papers, theses and dissertations.* New York: Modern Language Association.
Mullin, C. J. (1977). *A guide to writing and publishing in the social and behavioral sciences.* New York: John Wiley.
Pugh, G. T. (1963). *Guide to research writing.* Boston: Houghton Mifflin.

10 ✔

Computing: Using A
Personal Computer Effectively

TWO SCENARIOS

Both Jon and Ron began the dissertation process at about the same time. Neither were totally clear about the exact focus of their project, so both went to the library to examine the literature in their general area of interest, and both found themselves in the reference section. Jon asked his reference librarian what indexes and abstracts were available to locate journal articles, dissertations, reviews, and books. Following his librarian's advice Jon decided to examine PsychLIT, the compact disk (CD ROM) version of *Psychological Abstracts*. He typed in the name of his topic and discovered 234 articles published since 1966 in his general area of interest. He then narrowed his search by selecting only those articles dealing with one topic area that particularly interested him. He discovered that there were 36 articles that focused on this topic. This seemed a reasonable place to start, so Jon placed his floppy disk in the computer and copied the abstracts and references of the 36 articles onto this disk. He then went home to examine these on his personal computer. The total time involved was less than 30 minutes. Ron, on the other hand, began by locating the shelves containing the yearly volumes of Psychological Abstracts. Beginning with 1966 he pulled each volume from the shelf and searched for his topic. Six hours later Ron had obtained approximately the same information as Jon; however, he has also made 36 trips to the Xerox machine to copy the abstracts from each volume.

Later both Jon and Ron carefully examined the content of each abstract, Jon on the screen of his personal computer and Ron by examining the Xerox copies. Both determined that there were 10 articles that were worthy of a complete reading and both returned to the library. Ron and Jon each made Xerox copies of all ten articles. Once home each began to take notes. Jon used database management software designed for textual material. Ron used 3 × 5 index cards.[1]

Both Jon and Ron created a short literature review for the chair of their committee. Jon entered his review on his word processor while Ron used an electric typewriter. To make sure that his review was free from typing and grammatical errors, Jon used a spell checker and grammar checker to examine his document before letting his committee chair see it. Ron looked up most words he was unsure of in a dictionary, but he missed a few because he thought they were correct. Ron was unable to include a bibliography with his literature review because he did not have time to type all of the references from his 3 × 5 cards and place them in the correct format. Jon, on the other hand, simply instructed his database program to print the references in the appropriate format, an operation taking approximately 30 seconds.

Eventually both Jon and Ron were given approval to collect their data by their dissertation committee—Jon approximately 4 months before Ron. After collecting data, both decided to use the services of a statistical consultant to help with the computerized analysis of the data. Jon obtained all of his output in both hard copy (i.e., on paper) and on a floppy disk. Ron received only the hard copy. After deciding which output would serve as the basis for the tabular presentation, Jon was able to access this information with his word processor and add the necessary titles and labels. Jon, working from the hard copy, typed all of the information onto separate pages. Once again, Ron spent many more hours than Jon completing this stage of the process.

Finally, both Jon and Ron reached the final draft stage. Jon used a computer program to guarantee that every article cited in the dissertation was contained in the reference list and vice versa. He then had the list printed in the correct format. Ron, however, had to examine each reference on every page to make sure that the reference was included in the bibliography. Then he had to retype the list, including all the articles cited, in the correct format, using his 3 × 5 cards.

Both Jon and Ron finished their dissertation and both produced high quality work. Jon finished 8 months earlier than Ron. Despite spending considerable money and time learning how to use a number of different software programs, and the initial investment in a computer, Jon saved 8 months of tuition, which more than made up for the cost of his computer. Jon was able to give more time to the intellectual and creative aspects of his dissertation because the clerical and repetitive tasks were made easier. His dissertation reflects the fact that he was able to spend more time thinking about the content issues and less about format issues.

Finally, Jon brings to the labor market a number of highly generalizable computer skills that can be used to publish his dissertation in the form of a book or articles, to conduct new research and to keep records, to write letters and memos, to keep track of clients, and to organize his complex life. Ron, on the other hand, remains computer illiterate, which renders him a dinosaur in the world of the 1990s.

The point of the above two scenarios is that the entire process of completing a dissertation, from the initial formulation of an idea, through the preparation of the final draft, complete with references in the correct format and margins to satisfy the university librarian, can be streamlined with the aid of your personal computer. Gone are the days when every draft required completely retyping an entire chapter. One no longer needs to check spelling with a hand-held dictionary or to look up synonyms in a thesaurus. References can be automatically formatted to any style desired and your computer will check to make sure that every reference in your dissertation has a corresponding reference in your bibliography. As one of our students states,

> I found that the electronic tools that I used kept me organized and motivated throughout the entire process over two years. The [MacIntosh computer] that I used was fun to use and intrinsically motivating as a thinking tool. . . . Appropriate computer technology . . . reduces the "unauthentic labor" associated with the entire process: that unnecessary effort that gets in the way of conceptualizing, organizing and presenting information. (Helen Barrett, personal communication)

This chapter is designed to provide you with information about the available software that performs these miracles of the computer age. We describe what the software does and how it may help you. We organize the chapter in a manner reflecting the organization of the dissertation process. We begin with suggestions on how to use the computer to assist with formulating an idea and reviewing the literature. Second, we review software for taking notes and controlling your bibliography. Third, we discuss the writing process, how to streamline your writing, check your spelling and grammar, and produce multiple revisions with little effort. Next we consider questions of data analysis. We review programs that perform both qualitative and quantitative analysis. Finally, we consider the costs of using the available technology in terms of the cost/benefit ratios involved in learning to use sophisticated software.

USING YOUR PC AS A LITERATURE SEARCHING TOOL: DIALOG AND KNOWLEDGE INDEX

The standard reply of a dissertation advisor when faced with a student's vague notions regarding a research topic is, "Go to the library and find out what information exists on this subject." A thorough literature review is an absolute requirement for a dissertation and can be the most time-consuming of all dissertation tasks.

The task before you is to obtain a comprehensive view of the literature relevant to your topic of interest. At the preliminary stages the most you probably want are references, and maybe abstracts, but only after much culling of information will you want complete articles. Computerized data bases, or "online search services," are ideal for this purpose. DIALOG and Knowledge Index are services of DIALOG Information Services, Inc. Knowledge Index, the easiest to use and less expensive of the two services, allows access most evenings after 6 p.m., and as of this writing requires an initial start up fee of $35.00 including two hours of free searching time (which costs $24.00/hour after that). As stated in their advertising brochure, Knowledge Index allows you to "locate just the information you need from millions of references covered in over 50,000 journals. No special equipment or programming skills are needed. Virtually any personal computer and a compatible modem will give you access to many of the same databases used by professional researchers" (Knowledge Index).

USING YOUR LIBRARY'S COMPUTERIZED SEARCH CAPABILITY

Most university libraries have moved to a search system that allows users, free of charge, to access reference materials from compact disks (CD ROM). Compact disks store the information from reference sources in a wide variety of disciplines and allow students and faculty to search topic areas and print out lists of references and abstracts related to their topic of interest. A few of the available CD ROM databases are described below.

ERIC (Educational Resources Information Clearinghouse): ERIC is a database of education-related materials collected by the Educational Resources Information Center of the U.S. Department of Education. ERIC covers books, reports, unpublished documents, and approximately 750 journals in education.

ABI INFORM: A database of business information consisting of bibliographic entries and abstracts to more than 800 different journals. The database includes the most recent five years and is an excellent source of information on companies, products, business conditions, management techniques, and so on.

PsychLIT: The PsychLIT database contains summaries of the world's literature in psychology and related disciplines and is compiled from material published in *Psychological Abstracts* and the Psych database. PsychLIT covers more than 1,400 journals in 29 different languages from approximately 54 countries. Note that the computerized version of an index or abstract may have a slightly different name than the print version. For example, *Psychological Abstracts* on CD ROM is called PsychLIT; online, it's called PsychInfo.

SOCIOFILE: The Sociofile database contains information from approximately 1,500 journals in 30 different languages from about 55 countries. It covers sociology and related disciplines by including bibliography citations and abstracts (from *Sociological Abstracts)* and enhanced dissertation citations from *Dissertation Abstracts International.*

SOCIAL SCIENCES INDEX: The SSI provides subject access to 300 major English-language periodicals published in the United States and abroad, in these and related areas of the social sciences: anthropology, black studies, economics, environmental sciences, geography, international relations, law and criminology, planning and public administration, political science, psychology, public health, sociology, urban studies, and women's studies.

The library card catalog is also becoming a thing of the past. Card catalogs are now maintained as computer databases, or "Online

Public Access Catalogs." These provide complete bibliographic information (e.g., author, title, publisher, date, etc.), location, call number, and circulation status of every item in the library. Even if you only know the approximate title, or part of the author's name, the online catalog will search for close approximations and return all references that come close. Most online catalogs can be searched from your personal computer via a modem and telecommunications software.

ADVANTAGES AND DISADVANTAGES OF COMPUTERIZED LITERATURE SEARCHING

There are both advantages and disadvantages of computerized search strategies as compared to the "old fashioned" method using printed indexes and abstracts. Clearly, using a computer speeds things up. Online indexes are also likely to be more up-to-date. Another big advantage is the ability of the computerized search to examine titles and abstracts for key words. For example, Mann (1987) notes that in the early 1980s *Psychological Abstracts* did not contain the word *burnout* as a heading or cross-reference, but searching for *burnout* as a key word produced more than 200 items in such varied areas as occupational stress, occupational adjustment, and employee attitudes.

Some databases also permit very unique search strategies that permit access to review articles, letters to the editor, articles written only in English, and articles written only after (or before) a certain date. Finally, computerized searches permit the crossing of terms. For example, if you are interested in suicide among adolescent males, a computerized search may permit the crossing of suicide with adolescent, with male (or gender).

Despite the tremendous advantages cited above, there are also some costs and frustrations likely to be encountered with computerized searches. First, online searching is not free. Second, you may want to search several databases, but each may need to be searched in a different manner as search processes are not necessarily the same across all databases. Third, books are not as likely to be referenced as journal articles and the indexing of books may not be as thorough. Fourth, older articles may no longer be referenced on computerized databases. For example, the print version of *Psychological Abstracts* covers from 1927, while the CD ROM version (PsychLIT) covers only from 1967. Fifth, if you hire a library search technician you are relinquishing control to another person, not as likely to understand your topic or its related terms. The potential for missed references is very real. Finally, searches may uncover articles containing the correct words, but in the wrong area. Mann (1987) mentions that a search to locate articles on "Venetian blinds" may also uncover references on "blind Venetians."

In sum, computerized reference location takes the drudgery out of finding what is available on a topic, but it is not a guarantee. A bad search can be conducted with the computer as well as without it. Like all aspects of the dissertation process, literature searching takes care and patience.

PERSONAL COMPUTING ENVIRONMENTS

As a personal computer user you will probably be working on equipment produced by IBM or a replication of the IBM method of computing (a "clone") or on equipment produced by Apple Computing, Inc. In reality the parts of a computer system are manufactured by many different companies, but IBM and Apple have largely defined the two major personal computing environments. The command-driven environment, represented by DOS and the graphic environment developed by Apple for the MacIntosh computer represent two extremely different methods of computing. As suggested by Barrett (1990), one system may provide a better "fit" to a student's method of thinking and learning than another. Recently, Microsoft has developed an environment known as Windows that allows IBM and IBM clones to utilize a "graphical user interface" similar to that used by Apple. We make no recommendations regarding which environment is best, other than to note that it is probably less expensive to become fully equipped in an IBM environment. The novice should talk to users of all three environments, consider the costs and benefits of each, their own learning style, the support offered by their university, and the equipment used by their faculty advisors and dissertation chair before making a choice.

READING AND RECORDING:
HOW TO TAKE NOTES WITH YOUR COMPUTER

Assume that you have obtained a list of articles that you wish to pursue in greater detail. As you begin reading these articles you will want to keep a record of the complete bibliographic reference, the major points, the methods of data collection and analysis, and so on. One method of doing this is with a database management program. The advantage of a database manager is that you can retrieve and reorder the information in a variety of ways. For example, a database manager designed for use with text-based material, such as Notebook II+,[2] can be used to record notes, to conduct content analyses, and to manage bibliographies. In the following paragraph we provide a more thorough description of the capabilities of Notebook II+.

Notebook II+ is a software package designed specifically for academic work. Entering information into a database is as easy as entering information into a word processor. Once notes (and bibliographic resources) are stored in a database, the power you have to organize and access them is dramatically increased. There are many forms that a database created with Notebook II+ may take. A note card database, for example, may contain as many or as few "headings" or fields as you find useful for your work. You might want to include, on each entry, the date on which the note was taken, the location of the source, the major variables being discussed, the type of research design used, the type of sample, and so on. Notes can be cross-referenced by any keywords you select, such as the names of sources, dates, topics, designs, variables, and more. You can set up as many fields as you like for "tagging" your records with keywords, and enter as many terms or phrases as you need in each of these fields. You can ask the program to prepare an alphabetical list of all the terms you've used. You can also instruct the program to produce a "keyword index" of your database. You can look for a word or phrase anywhere in your database. You can search all your references for notes covering a particular subject. You may also move notes created with Notebook II+ directly into your word processor, so you do not have to type them twice. You can print any portion of the information in your records, in just about any form you wish. For example, you could print notes on index cards. Finally, if you purchase Notebook II+ you are provided with a program called NB Citation, the most powerful bibliographic database utility available. It works with all major word processing packages and constructs bibliographies and reference lists in more than 700 publishing styles. The bibliographic database you keep with Notebook II+ stores information on books, journal articles, conference papers, and other works used in your research. When you are ready to submit your work the program will read though your word-processed document for citations and generate a bibliography or reference list. Author names, dates, titles, and so on will be placed in the proper sequence, presented in the correct form, and punctuated as a citation.

BIBLIOGRAPHIES: A SPECIAL CASE

Constructing bibliographies is a particularly troublesome and time-consuming aspect of any research. It is critical that bibliographies be in the correct format and contain the correct information, yet one of the most frequent complaints of those who read others' dissertations is that the references are incorrect.

Three methods for dealing with bibliographies are currently available. First, some word processors, such as Note Bene, and the APA word processor Manuscript Manager, are designed for professional writing and have built-in methods for handling citations and bibliographic references. Second, some database managers have the ability to format bibliographic information. Third, some programs are designed specifically for professional researchers to aid with the referencing process. A particularly good program, designed exclusively for the management of bibliographies, is Papyrus. The paragraph below provides a complete description of this program. Although Papyrus does not have the additional capabilities of Notebook II+, it is considerably cheaper.

Papyrus, by Reference Systems, is billed as "The New Standard in Bibliographic Databases." According to the literature available about Papyrus, you are able to "store up to 2 million references of up to 16,000 characters, plus 100 key words each." "References may be stored manually or imported from online databases such as DIALOG [and Knowledge Index], services such as Current Contents on Diskette, other personal bibliography systems, and existing text files."

> The program produces references in any desired format. Numerous predefined journal formats are supplied and additional formats can easily be created by modifying one of the predefined formats or by designing your own. Papyrus helps you build a personal database of literature citations, abstracts, and notes that can be used to automatically produce flawless bibliographies. After you prepare a manuscript Papyrus searches the text for citations, inserts the correct citation format in the text, and produces a bibliography ready for printing in the style you specify. (Papyrus: The new standard in personal bibliographic databases)

WRITING AND SPELLING

Faculty members like to talk about the "old days" when we had to continually type and retype each chapter numerous times to please the whims of every member of a dissertation committee. A high proportion of the total time involved in producing the final product was consumed with these chores. Word processing has changed the process drastically, and for the better. It is not reasonable or sensible to undertake any major writing task, particularly a dissertation, without a word processor. Word processing takes care of the writing, spelling, formatting, rewriting, and rearranging needs of the writer. In addition, most word-processing programs offer synonyms to words at the touch of a key (i.e., a computerized thesaurus).

There are many word-processing programs and most are more than capable of handling a dissertation. The two most widely used are WordPerfect and Microsoft Word. Both Microsoft Word and WordPerfect are available in DOS, Windows, and MacIntosh environments and both have conversion programs that allow the user to convert from one word-processing format to another. Both programs offer spell checking and a thesaurus and WordPerfect offers a British and French dictionary and thesaurus. Both programs will create outlines, generate indexes, tables of contents, footnotes, and annotations. WordPerfect has an equation editor that permits development of complex mathematical expressions. Both programs have the ability to incorporate graphics produced by other programs into their text. With WordPerfect you are also able to move, rotate, and scale graphics to your demands.

Given the wide variety of features you might think that the programs are difficult to learn, but that is not the case. The learning curve is very fast and one can be "up and running" in a short time. As you become more sophisticated you can master the variety of special skills that allow you to polish and manipulate your manuscript. In addition, user guides and manuals are available from most bookstores, which provide additional help beyond that offered by the manuals that come with the software.

There are dozens of other word-processing programs that we could describe, but our purpose has been to give you an overview of word-processing power, not a review of all software. In Box 10.1 we briefly mention some of the other available programs.

Box 10.1

WORD PROCESSING SOFTWARE: An Overview

PROGRAM NAME (DOS, MAC, Windows)	MANUFACTURER
WordPerfect DOS MAC Windows	WordPerfect Corp.
Microsoft Word DOS MAC Windows	Microsoft
WordStar DOS Windows	WordStar International
Ami Professional Windows	Samma Corp.
Multi-Mate DOS	Ashton-Tate
FullWrite Prof. MAC	Ashton-Tate
Mindreader DOS, Windows	Brown Bag Software
MacWrite II MAC	Claris Corp.
Bank Street Writer DOS	Broderbund Software

NOTE: For a review of 56 word-processing programs see "Word Processing," by Patrick Honan and Joseph Devlin, *Personal Computing*, August, 1990. Above prices are approximations, least expensive prices are usually found at college bookstores and through mail order. Version numbers have been left off. Make sure that you have purchased the most recent version of any software.

HOWS YOU'RE GRAMMER?

Note that there are three errors in the heading to this section. "Hows" should be "How is." "You're" should be "your," and "grammer" is spelled incorrectly (grammar). A grammar-checking program would detect all three errors, while a spell checker would miss the inappropriate use of "You're." Grammar checkers are extremely useful programs and are constantly being improved. As of this writing the major competitors are Grammatik, Right Writer, and Correct Grammar. All of these programs will check your document for grammatical errors, some without leaving your word-processing program. In addition your writing will be evaluated for clarity and reading level; and the program will check your writing against a standard. For example, Grammatik provides a comparison of your writing with the Gettysburg Address, a Hemingway short story, and an insurance policy.

A relatively recent addition to the available programs that evaluate writing is Corporate Voice. Corporate Voice moves beyond mechanical and grammatical writing problems to address the analysis of rhythm, cadence, and style. With Corporate Voice writers can select the style they wish to replicate and "fine tune" their own style to match the standard they select. For example, if you used the writing style exemplified by major journals in your discipline or the articles written by your dissertation chair as a standard, Corporate Voice would allow you to adjust your own writing to approximate these standards. At more than $200.00 Corporate Voice is considerably more expensive than other grammar checking programs, but for the good writer this program may provide the opportunity to move beyond mere grammar to the development of a style that fits the intended audience.

SHOULD I CONDUCT MY OWN STATISTICAL ANALYSIS?

The scariest part of the dissertation for many students is statistical analysis. There are many reasons for this. First, statistics are frequently equated with mathematics and many behavioral scientists feel incompetent with mathematics. Incompetence with math may generalize to similar feelings of helplessness with statistics. Second, statistics is viewed as the purview of a relatively few "high priests" who are the only ones who can understand it. The average person is not supposed to understand statistics. Third, statistics courses often reinforce students' beliefs regarding the intractability of statistics. Statistics is typically taught in the abstract. Statistics courses may focus on mathematical proofs, require the memorization of formulas, and rest heavily on probability theory.

The truth of the matter is that statistics is merely a tool. While it is true that statistics must be "calculated," and thus require mathematics, virtually no one calculates statistics. Calculation is a job best left to computers. Statistics are only meaningful when applied to a particular question. It is our experience that when students are fully aware of what that question is, they are able to understand, and discuss, the sorts of answers to that question that statistics provide. Just as one does not need to understand the internal combustion engine to drive a car, or the silicon chip to operate a computer, one does not need a strong mathematical background to use statistics in an efficient and intelligent manner.

Given the above points, how does one learn enough about statistics to use them as a tool in the dissertation process? There are a number of answers to this question, and the answer often depends on the nature of the institution that a student is attending. Students at large research universities will be required to take a number of statistics and computer courses, will often serve as research assistants on faculty projects, and will be trained in a tradition of research that requires the mastery of quantitative analysis to achieve success. These students will frequently approach the dissertation with sufficient experience, and enough additional sources of expertise, to analyze and interpret their dissertation data.

But what about everybody else? For these people there are a number of sources of assistance. A patient and understanding faculty member may play the role of "statistical educator." It is a good idea to select a committee that contains at least one person willing to be of assistance with analytical issues. Second, independent reading is often of value. Many students "model" their analyses on the basis of similar analyses done by others. By reading how one person presents the results of analysis of variance or regression analysis, students learn how to present their own. There are many texts that do a good job of presenting elementary statistics to students, but only a few that present complex multivariate methods in a clear, intuitive manner. One of the best of these is Sam Kash Kachigan's *Statistical Analysis: An Interdisciplinary Introduction to Univariate and Multivariate Methods* (1986).

SHOULD I BUY MY OWN STATISTICS PROGRAM?

The three main statistics packages are SPSS (Statistical Package for the Social Sciences), SAS (Statistical Analysis System) and BMDP

(BioMedical Data Programs). All three are available on very large computers found at universities (Mainframe and Minicomputers) and on personal computers. There are also other programs available for the personal computer, such as Stata, GB Stat, SysStat, and StatPac Gold, that can conduct most major analyses. Be very careful about purchasing a small, less sophisticated package available for the personal computer. Often these are so limited as to make very simple changes very time consuming, and thus very expensive. The problem with inexpensive programs, as mentioned above, is that they reach their limitations very quickly. You need to think ahead about flexibility, which is very difficult to do if you are not very experienced. It is a mistake to spend a lot of time learning a program that has little flexibility. The large statistical packages, such as SPSS, permit incredible flexibility in terms of what you can do with your data. They have the ability to handle a very large amount of data with thousands of cases and hundreds of variables. The problem is that these programs are quite expensive. Some universities have site licenses that permit faculty and students to copy statistical software, or have negotiated purchase agreements that reduce the costs. One of the most important points about statistical software decisions is to use what your department recommends and your chair is familiar with.

WHAT ABOUT QUALITATIVE DATA ANALYSIS?

Qualitative data analysis can be greatly facilitated by the use of computer software. Qualitative analysis software, such as The Ethnograph for the IBM environment and QualPro for the MacIntosh environment, allows the researcher to code segments of text and later retrieve all the text given any common code, or combinations of codes. For example, one of the authors recently completed a study of social workers' attitudes toward prepaid health care. Prior to any use of the computer, all interviews were coded by county, question number, and job assignment. Interview text was then coded and recoded, individually and in group meetings, until a comprehensive coding system was developed. This code system was then used with The Ethnograph to code all interview transcripts. Only after this process had been completed was it possible to reorganize the text based on rules built into the coding system. Though The Ethnograph has the ability to reorganize text in multiple ways, the "analysis" rests almost entirely on the sophistication of the code system built by the researcher. In qualitative analysis the "organizing frame-work" must be rebuilt by each analyst approaching a new body of textural material.

UTILITIES: SOFTWARE TO STREAMLINE AND PROTECT YOUR SYSTEM

Disk utility libraries or "utilities" are special software programs designed to make living with your computer easier. They allow you to perform hundreds of operations that facilitate working with DOS, such as making the copying of files easier, evaluating the status of your entire system, checking disks and files for errors, and recovering files that have been inadvertently deleted. Another advantage of utility programs is that you can create menus that appear on the screen when you "boot-up" (i.e., turn on) your computer. A menu display will allow you to enter the software program of your choice at the touch of a key. While there are hundreds of utilities available, two programs, which are really integrated packages of dozens of utilities, stand out as superior: Norton Utilities and PC Tools Deluxe. We briefly describe each below.

The Norton Utilities, designed by Peter Norton, is a group of programs designed for both the technically sophisticated computer user and the novice. Two of the most appealing utilities are those that allow formatting of a floppy disk from an easy to understand screen menu, and the ability to find a file containing a string of text. For example, if your computer contains hundreds of files, but you want the one you created two years ago about Bureaucratic Structure in Complex Organizations, Norton Utilities will search every file for the text string "Bureaucratic Structure" and report all files that contain those words. The Norton Utilities also allow you to control system hardware by setting the screen colors, speed of the cursor, and other system attributes. You can test floppy and hard disks for physical errors and fix some of these, thus saving your files. With the Norton Utilities you can display technical information about a disk and undo the accidental formatting of a disk. The Norton Utilities will also recover an accidentally deleted file, a nifty little trick when you need it. These are only some of the things Norton Utilities will do, and though not directly relevant to the job of getting the dissertation done, the ability of these programs to repair your drastic mistakes makes them almost a necessity.

PC Tools Deluxe is another package of utilities, some of which overlap with the Norton Utilities and some of which are unique. One of the attractive features is the "desktop manager," which includes a notepad, appointment scheduler, auto-dialer, and calculator. Also beneficial are the hard disk backup utilities that allow you to back up and update the files on your hard disk in case of a disk crash (very disturbing when your dissertation chapters are all stored on the hard disk). Finally, PC Tools Deluxe includes a "DOS Shell," a set of programs that perform DOS functions, only more simply and easily. All of these functions, and many that are not mentioned above, make PC Tools Deluxe the top-rated utility program by *PC World* for the IBM environment (Lauriston, 1990). If you only buy one utility library, PC Tools Deluxe is the one to buy.

HOW MUCH COMPUTER DO I NEED?

Computer technology is changing at a tremendous rate and it is risky to make recommendations regarding what a student or colleague needs today, when these are likely to change tomorrow. There are a few basic questions that a potential consumer should ask before even starting to look for a computer system. We feel that the most essential of these is, "What computer configuration is being used by my department and my committee members?" A second, related question is, "What computer software is my committee familiar with?" It is very important to be "compatible" with your academic department and committee. This allows you to seek advice regarding the use of software and the interpretation of computer output, particularly from statistical programs.

A person about to purchase a computer should be aware of what his or her minimum needs are likely to be in each of the following areas.

Microprocessor. The microprocessor is the "chip" that actually performs the analyses, manipulates the data, and is the central component to any computer system. You should be able to specify the chip that you will need to work quickly and effectively with the software you wish to use.

Disk Drives. A computer MUST have a hard disk and at least one floppy disk. The storage requirements (expressed as megabytes or MB) for hard disk drives are increasing rapidly. Only recently a

20MB hard disk seemed quite adequate; however, currently popular programs may consume more than half—10MB—of that space. Computer memory stored on compact disks (CD ROM) is likely to replace or augment the hard disk drive and can add hundreds of megabytes of information to a computer system.

Random Access Memory (RAM). Random access memory is electronic memory that is used to store portions of programs needed for immediate use, including parts of the operating system. This memory is "volatile" in the sense that once you turn off your computer all information stored in RAM is erased. You should be aware of how much random access memory is needed to access the programs you plan to use.

Screen Display. How much resolution is needed for you to work without eye strain and to get the best possible use of your software? Do you need a "color" screen? What type of display works best with your software? The choice of a monitor can be one of the most important decisions in choosing a system. (After all, you will have to stare at it for thousands of hours.)

Mouse. A "mouse" is a device that allows you to "point" at things on the screen by moving the mouse on your desk and "clicking" to select certain options from the screen. A good deal of today's software requires a mouse to function effectively.

Printer. Without a printer you will have no printed output. Laser printers provide the cleanest, quietest, fastest output, but are also the most expensive. If you can afford it, a personal laser printer is a good investment. Dot matrix printers can also produce very nice output, but check the speed and print quality of the printer you are considering. A good dot matrix printer, with 24 pins (which produce the image on the page) should be obtainable for less than $300.00. (Most libraries will not accept dot matrix output in a final dissertation draft.)

Modem. A modem is a device that allows your computer to communicate with other computers. A modem is necessary to communicate with DIALOG or Knowledge Index, your University Library or Mainframe Computers in other locations. You will not be able to communicate with services such as Compuserve or Prodigy without a modem.

Math Co-Processor. A math co-processor is another chip that works together with your main microprocessor to speed up mathematical operations. As computer technology develops, such a co-processor may be included in the circuitry of the main chip and thus not necessary.

Other Options. Among the other available options are FAX boards; scanners to scan text, photographs, and graphs into a computer file; and devices for playing computer games and adding sound. While these are only peripherally useful for the dissertation, they may make your computer more "fun."

THE GUARANTEE: AN ESSENTIAL COMPONENT

Never buy a computer without a written guarantee. We think that a good guarantee should cover parts and labor for one year after purchase. We recommend against buying a computer with only a 90-day guarantee. One reason for buying a computer from an established vendor (Price Club, Circuit City, Best, Comp USA, Dell) is that they are likely to remain in business. A guarantee is only as good as the stability of the company that supports it. Computers assembled in someone's garage often work fine, but when they "crash" most computer dealers refuse to touch them.

IS IT REALLY WORTH IT?

A recommendation to spend a considerable sum of money may seem overwhelming to a student barely able to afford books; however, we feel that the computer is a tool that pays for itself very quickly. Many vendors are willing to set up a time payment system that can accommodate a student's income. Shop around and find a dealer who is willing to work out a payment plan. The computer business is very competitive and it's a buyers market.

SHOULD I COPY MY FRIEND'S PROGRAM AND SAVE SOME MONEY?

Many people will obtain a "bootlegged" program from a friend or acquaintance who happens to have a copy of a program they desire to own. This is not a particularly difficult thing to do because most software manufacturers have responded favorably to consumers' complaints regarding the difficulty of making backup copies and installing "copy-protected" software. We recommend against the copying of licensed software on moral, legal, and practical grounds. Morally speaking, the copying of software is taking the intellectual creativity, time, and money of another person without paying for it. This is no different than recording the music, copying the writing, or videotaping the films of another person. Second, copying of software is illegal. One is not simply copying software, one is *illegally* copying software. Third, software needs documentation. Copying software does not provide the documentation needed to install, run, troubleshoot, and understand the capabilities of the program. Fourth, software copied illegally may be contaminated by a "virus." A virus is a hidden program that "infects" a computer system, often doing very nasty things, such as erasing all files on the hard disk. When software is "passed around" the probability of picking up one of these viruses increases. Fifth, software copied illegally has no user support or guarantees. When you purchase software you will be asked to send in a license agreement. This agreement guarantees your program against "bugs," and allows the vendor to communicate with you regarding updates, add-on enhancements, and other related programs. In some cases the agreement also permits phone assistance, usually free, sometimes for a fee. In sum, buy your own software and feel good about it.

NOTES

1. If Jon had searched online using Knowledge Index or DIALOG he could have ordered the journal articles through DIALOG's document delivery service. This is a fairly expensive alternative, but takes only a few days.

2. Notebook II+ is available from Oberon Resources, 147 East Oakland, Columbus, Ohio 43201-1208. Tel. 1-800-594-9062.

11 ✔

Guidelines for the Presentation of Numbers in the Dissertation

Many dissertations require that the manuscript be typed in the format of the professional association representing the discipline of the dissertation. For example, in a department of psychology it is likely that the dissertation will present tables and figures, and describe these in the text, using guidelines required by the American Psychological Association (APA). This section describes the rules that one is likely to encounter when discussing numbers in text. Numbers may be expressed as words (five) or as figures (5), but when do we use a word as opposed to a figure? This section addresses nine areas of concern as outlined by the *Publication Manual of the American Psychological Association* (1983). We use the guidelines presented by the APA because they are complete, likely to cover a wide range of issues, and not idiosyncratic to just psychology.

EXPRESSING NUMBERS AS FIGURES

General Rule: Use figures to express numbers 10 and above and words to express numbers below 10 (APA, 1983).

EXAMPLES:

Correct	*Incorrect*
only about 13%	only about thirteen percent
a 22 mm line	a twenty-two millimeter line
four subjects	4 subjects
three out of five groups	3 out of 5 groups

EXCEPTIONS:

1. All numbers below 10 that are grouped for comparison with numbers 10 and above, and appear in the same paragraph, are also expressed as figures (APA, 1983).

Correct	*Incorrect*
5 of 32 groups	five of 32 groups
	five of thirty-two groups
when ranked, the 3rd and 12th	when ranked, the third and twelfth
	when ranked, the third and 12th
8 of the 30 cases	eight of the 30 cases
	eight of the thirty cases

2. Numbers that immediately precede a unit of measurement are expressed as figures, regardless of size (APA, 1983).

Correct	*Incorrect*
a 5 mm line	a five millimeter line
	a five mm line
a mean of 36.22 cm	a mean of thirty-six and twenty-two one hundredths centimeters

3. Numbers that represent statistical or mathematical functions, fractional or decimal quantities, percentages, ratios, and percentiles and quartiles are expressed as figures, regardless of size (APA, 1983).

Correct	*Incorrect*
a mean of 3.54	a mean of three point fifty four
	a mean of three and fifty-four one hundredths
subtracted from 5	subtracted from five

4 3/4 times as many	four and three fourths times as many
0.44	point forty-four
	.44 (must precede a decimal with 0)
a 5 kg weight	a five kilogram weight
scored in the 4th percentile	scored in the fourth percentile

4. Numbers that represent time, dates, ages, sample or population size, scores and points on a scale, exact sums of money, and numerals as numerals are expressed as figures, regardless of size (APA, 1983).

Correct	*Incorrect*
4 persons in each sample	four persons in each sample
seven 9 year old children	seven nine year old children
	7 9 year old children
in 7 years	in seven years
study began in 1984	study began in nineteen eighty-four
prior to April 1	prior to April first
no group lasted longer	no group lasted longer than
than 3.5 hours	three and one half hours
a score of 6 or greater	a score of six or greater
each subject was paid $7.50	each subject was paid seven
	dollars and fifty cents

5. Numbers that denote a specific place in a numbered series, parts of books and tables, each number in a list of four or more numbers are expressed as figures, regardless of size (APA, 1983).

Correct	*Incorrect*
sample 4	sample four
Figure 1	Figure One
page 60	Page sixty
Chapters 2, 5, 6, 8 and 23	Chapters two, five, six, eight and 23

EXPRESSING NUMBERS AS WORDS

General Rule: Use words to express numbers below 10 that do not represent precise measurements and that are not grouped for comparison with numbers 10 and above (APA, 1983).

EXAMPLES:

Correct	*Incorrect*
about seven or eight	about 7 or 8
one of the first	1 of the first
	1 of the 1st
only two persons	only 2 persons
two surveys	2 surveys
one-way ANOVA	1-way ANOVA
two-tailed F test	2-tailed F test

EXCEPTIONS:

1. The numbers *zero* and *one* when the words would be easier to comprehend than the figures or when the words do not appear in context with numbers 10 and above, are expressed in words (APA, 1983).

Correct	*Incorrect*
one-on-one session	1 on 1 session
only one subject	only 1 subject
the concept of zero	the concept of 0

2. Any number that begins a sentence, title, or heading should be expressed in words. (Whenever possible, reword the sentence to avoid beginning with a number [APA, 1983]).

Correct	*Incorrect*
Five studies support	5 studies support
Twenty-six percent of . . .	26% of . . .
	Twenty-six % of . . .

3. Common fractions are expressed as words (APA, 1983).

Correct	*Incorrect*
one half the sample	1/2 the sample
	1 half the sample
exactly one fifth	exactly 1/5

4. Honor universally accepted usage (APA, 1983).

| *Correct* | *Incorrect* |
| the Twelve Apostles | the 12 Apostles |

the Ten Commandments   the 10 Commandments
the Fourth of July   the 4th of July

COMBINING FIGURES AND WORDS
TO EXPRESS NUMBERS

General Rule: Use a combination of figures and words to express rounded large numbers and back-to-back modifiers (APA, 1983).

EXAMPLES: Rounded Large Numbers

Correct   *Incorrect*
About 3 thousand   About 3,000
                                     About three thousand

A net loss of $1 billion   A net loss of one-billion dollars
                                     a net lost of $1,000,000

EXAMPLES: Back-to-Back Modifiers

Correct   *Incorrect*
3 one-way interactions   three one-way interactions
2 two dollar bills   2 $2.00 bills
                                     2 2 dollar bills

ORDINAL NUMBERS

General Rule: Treat ordinal numbers (except percentiles and quartiles) as you would cardinal numbers (APA, 1983).

EXAMPLES:

Correct   *Incorrect*
the first sample   the 1st sample
the 11th grade   the eleventh grade
the 2nd and 12th   the second and 12th
                                     the second and twelfth

the second   the 2nd
the 12th   the twelfth

DECIMAL FRACTIONS

General Rule: Place the decimal point on the line, not above the line. Use a zero before the decimal point when numbers are less than 1 (APA, 1983).

EXAMPLES:

Correct	*Incorrect*
0.45 mm	point forty-five millimeters
	.45 mm
a 0.2 s interval	a .2 second interval

EXCEPTION: Do not use a zero before a decimal fraction when the number cannot be greater than 1, as in correlations, probability values, proportions, and levels of statistical significance (APA, 1983).

$r = .44, p < .01.$

ARABIC OR ROMAN NUMERALS

General Rule: Use Arabic, not Roman, numerals whenever possible (APA, 1983).

EXCEPTION: If Roman numerals are part of an established terminology, do not change to Arabic numbers; for example, use "Type II" error (APA, 1983).

COMMAS

General Rule: Use commas between groups of three digits in most figures of 1,000 or more (APA, 1983).

EXCEPTIONS:	*Correct*
Page numbers	page 2134
Binary Digits	001101010

Serial Numbers	571606999
Degrees of Temperature	2349° F
Acoustic Frequency Designations	3000 Hz
Degrees of Freedom	$F(35, 1100)$
Numbers to the right of a decimal point	6,750.0748

PLURALS OF NUMBERS

General Rule: To form the plurals of numbers, whether expressed as figures or as words, add s or es alone, without an apostrophe (APA, 1983).

EXAMPLES:

Correct	*Incorrect*
the early 1960s	the early 1960's
from the 30s and 40s	from the 30's and 40's

APA REQUIREMENTS FOR STATISTICAL AND MATHEMATICAL COPY

1. Your Responsibilities

You are responsible for selecting the correct statistical method and the accuracy of all supporting data. Raw data should be retained for 5 years following publication (APA, 1983).

2. Should References for Statistical Analyses be Presented?

Statistics in common use are not referenced. Less common statistics not commonly found in textbooks should be referenced. When a statistic is used in a unique or controversial manner, or when the statistic is itself the focus of the research, references should be given (APA, 1983).

3. Presenting Inferential Statistics in Text

Give the symbol, degrees of freedom, value, and probability level. In addition, give the mean or other descriptive statistic to clarify the nature of the effect (APA, 1983).

EXAMPLES: *F* and *t* tests

$F(2, 34) = 67.22, p < .001$
$t(35) = 3.71, p < .001$

EXAMPLES: Chi-Square Statistics

$\chi^2(4, N = 78) = 11.15, p < .05$

4. Should symbols or word terms be used in the text?

Use the term, not the symbol (APA, 1983).

EXAMPLES:

Correct	*Incorrect*
The means were	The Ms were
	The Xs were
The standard deviations were	The SDs were

5. How do I express the number of subjects?

Use an uppercase underlined *N* to designate the number of members in the total sample and a lowercase underlined *n* to designate the number of members in a limited portion of the total sample (APA, 1983).

EXAMPLES:

a total sample of $N = 130$
$n = 50$ in each group

6. How do I express percentages?

Use the symbol for percent only when it is preceded by a numeral. Use the word percentage when a number is not given (APA, 1983).

EXAMPLES:

21% of the sample
the percentage of the sample that

EXCEPTION: In table and figure headings and legends use the % symbol to conserve space (APA, 1983).

This completes our discussion of the presentation of numbers in text, but the details of APA and other formats include considerably more than just the above set of rules. In addition, the American Psychological Association has an excellent guide to assist students with the use of the APA publication manual. *Mastering APA Style: Student's Workbook and Training Guide* (1990) includes instruction and exercises covering references and citations, tables, statistical and mathematical copy, and other topics.

Finally, it is advisable to begin using your discipline's style at the very beginning of the dissertation process. This gives you considerable time to master the intricacies of the style, and prevents you from having to "fix" hundreds of pages of text at the very end.

12 ✔

Informed Consent and
Other Ethical Concerns

All universities have ethical standards for conducting research with human beings, most have formally established "human subjects committees," and many have institutionalized procedures to guarantee that informed consent is obtained prior to initiating all research. It is the student's responsibility to become knowledgeable about the university's requirements, obtain the necessary documentation, and follow the university's guidelines. This should be done prior to collecting data, as early as possible after the research procedures are established. One important reason for meeting these expectations in a timely fashion is that you may be required to obtain an authorizing signature from the human subjects committee and these committees tend not to meet very often.

COMMON ETHICAL CONCERNS

The two main ethical issues that pertain to using subjects in social science research are the need for fully informed consent to participate and the need to emerge from the experience unharmed. Ultimately, the value of a study is determined by balancing the potential benefits, in terms of generalizable knowledge, with the costs and potential risks. A recurrent problem is the failure of students to reflect conscientiously upon how particular subjects are likely to experience the study. One cannot cavalierly assume that experimental manipulations, interviews, questionnaires, or even feedback of results, will not be upsetting to some participants. It is permissible for research to carry some risk, but it is imperative to anticipate such risks beforehand.

Perhaps the most controversial type of research design is one that employs concealment or deception. The issue here is whether more straightforward, alternative procedures are available and whether the deception is justified by the theoretical or applied value of the study. Field studies may raise important ethical concerns when the investigator deviously manipulates variables in the environment or when a research component is covertly introduced into an everyday situation, such as gathering data from unwitting employees in the course of their jobs. The rule here is to seek informed consent whenever there is more than minimal risk of harm to the participants. In any case, full disclosure needs to be given to participants as soon as possible after the data have been obtained. Over the course of time the biggest drawback to the use of concealment or deception is probably the gradual erosion of public trust in the research enterprise.

The American Psychological Association has a clearly stated set of guidelines for "Research with Human Participants." We reproduce these guidelines in their entirety in Box 12.1. Other disciplines may operate with somewhat different standards, but this is a relatively complete list that well represents the ethical concerns voiced by researchers in the social sciences. The APA guidelines form the foundation for obtaining informed consent according to the 11 points discussed below.

INFORMED CONSENT

One key element of conducting ethical research involves obtaining informed consent from your participants. Informed consent is required in most cases, unless there is "minimal risk." Examples of methodologies that typically do not require informed consent include secondary analyses of data, archival research, and the systematic observation of publicly observable data, such as shoppers in a suburban mall. There is some lack of clarity and need for judgment about the standard of minimal risk. For example, the criterion of

Box 12.1

ETHICAL PRINCIPLES OF PSYCHOLOGISTS
Principle 9

Research With Human Participants

The decision to undertake research rests upon a considered judgment by the individual psychologist about how best to contribute to psychological science and human welfare. Having made the decision to conduct research, the psychologist considers alternative directions in which research energies and resources might be invested. On the basis of this consideration, the psychologist carries out the investigation with respect and concern for the dignity and welfare of the people who participate and with cognizance of federal and state regulations and professional standards governing the conduct of research with human participants.

a. In planning a study, the investigator has the responsibility to make a careful evaluation of its ethical acceptability. To the extent that the weighing of scientific and human values suggests a compromise of any principle, the investigator incurs a correspondingly serious obligation to seek ethical advice and to observe stringent safeguards to protect the rights of human participants.

b. Considering whether a participant in a planned study will be a "subject at risk" or a "subject at minimal risk," according to recognized standards, is of primary ethical concern to the investigator.

c. The investigator always retains the responsibility for ensuring ethical practice in research. The investigator is also responsible for the ethical treatment of participants by collaborators, assistants, students and employees, all of whom, however, incur similar obligations.

d. Except in minimal-risk research, the investigator establishes a clear and fair agreement with research participants, prior to their participation, that clarifies the obligations and responsibilities of each. The investigator has the obligation to honor all promises and commitments included in that agreement. The investigator informs the participants of all aspects of the research that might reasonably be expected to influence willingness to participate and explains all other aspects of the research about which the participants inquire. Failure to make full disclosure prior to obtaining informed consent requires additional safeguards to protect the welfare and dignity of the research participants. Research with children or with participants who have impairments that would limit understanding and/or communication requires special safeguarding procedures.

e. Methodological requirements of a study may make the use of concealment or deception necessary. Before conducting such a study, the investigator has a special responsibility to (i) determine whether the use of such techniques is justified by the study's prospective scientific, educational, or applied value; (ii) determine whether alternative procedures are available that do not use concealment or deception; and (iii) ensure that the participants are provided with sufficient explanation as soon as possible.

f. The investigator respects the individual's freedom to decline to participate in or to withdraw from the research at any time. The obligation to pretest this freedom requires careful thought and consideration when the investigator is in a position of authority or influence over the participant. Such positions of authority include, but are not limited to, situations in which research participation is required as part of employment or in which the participant is a student, client, or employee of the investigator.

g. The investigator protects the participant from physical and mental discomfort, harm, and danger that may arise from research procedures. If risks of such consequences exist, the investigator informs the participant of that fact. Research procedures likely to cause serious or lasting harm to a participant are not used unless the failure to use these procedures might expose the participant to risk of greater harm, or unless the research has great potential benefit and fully informed and voluntary consent is obtained from each participant. The participant should be informed of procedures for contacting the investigator within a reasonable time period following participation should stress, potential harm, or related questions or concerns arise.

h. After the data are collected, the investigator provides the participant with information about the nature of the study and attempts to remove any misconceptions that may have arisen. Where scientific or humane values justify delaying or withholding this information, the investigator incurs a special responsibility to monitor the research and to ensure that there are no damaging consequences for the participant.

i. Where research procedures result in undesirable consequences for the individual participant, the investigator has the responsibility to detect and remove or correct these consequences, including long-term effects.

j. Information obtained about a research participant during the course of an investigation is confidential unless otherwise agreed upon in advance. When the possibility exists that others may obtain access to such information, this possibility, together with the plans for protecting confidentiality, is explained to the participant as part of the procedure for obtaining informed consent.

minimal risk could pertain to research involving brief questionnaires that do not address questions likely to be disturbing to the participants. Questions regarding favored sports or preferred television programs are probably not disturbing; questions regarding childhood victimization probably are. The elements of informed consent are outlined below:

Tell the participant who is conducting the study.

This is usually the student; however, other persons, such as friends, spouses, or paid employees may also be used to collect data.

Why was the particular person singled out for participation?

Answer the "Why me?" question. For example, "You have been selected to participate in this project because you have recently experienced the birth of your first child. We are particularly interested in your experience of . . ."

What is the time commitment?

Let the participant know about how long it will take to complete his or her involvement. For example, "Pretesting with these instruments indicates that it takes approximately 45 minutes to complete all forms."

Are there any benefits to be expected?

Be reasonable, but don't oversell the study. Typically, there are few or no advantages to participating in most research. Hopefully, the person will feel good about helping someone collect data, but this is not a particular benefit.

Are there any potential risks, and how have these been managed?

Let the participants know what the potential risks are. What will you offer participants who experience difficulties attributable to participating in your study? For example, "Some people may experience negative emotions when discussing parental alcoholism. If you would like to discuss these with someone please feel free to call the study director at the number below." In the case of studies with no foreseeable risks, "There are no known risks associated with participation in this research."

Explain the study and offer to answer questions.

This should be done in lay language easily understood by your subject population. If you cannot share the purpose of the study fully because it would compromise the integrity of the research, describe what the subject is expected to do and provide the purpose during the debriefing. Offer to answer questions about the study then.

Participation is always voluntary.

Subjects should not be subtly pressured to participate by your assumption of social status or the scientific establishment to lend more authority to the project. Moreover, the participant has a right to withdraw from the study at any time.

When conducting research in any setting where the participant is likely to experience pressure to participate, it is important to make this point explicit. For example, "Your participation in this research is not required and will have no effect on your grade in this course. You may choose to withdraw from the research at any time without penalty." In some settings a person may be apprehensive that his or her social standing, job security, or friendships would be affected by participating or by not participating. In these situations it is of particular importance that decisions to participate, to decline to participate, and to withdraw be confidential.

Provide the participants with a copy of the informed consent form.

The participant should be given a copy of the "informed consent form" (if relevant) and asked to sign another copy for the researcher. For example, "If you would like to participate in this study please sign one copy of the attached consent form and return it in the enclosed envelope. Keep the other copy for your records."

Payment

Will the subject receive compensation for participation? Let the subject know what payment he or she can expect, if any.

Confidentiality

Let the subject know the limits of confidentiality. Confidentiality is different from anonymity. Confidentiality means that *no one,* including the researcher, will know your identity. Anonymity means that your identity will be preserved, at all costs, by the researcher. For example, if your data are transcribed or analyzed by a third party, how can you guarantee confidentiality? Typically, summary statistics based on data will be public. In funded research the data may also be public, but identifying information is removed, and there are either too many data, or to little information, to identify individuals.

Debriefing

If there is to be a debriefing, let the participant know how you will do it. You may choose to describe the purpose of the study in more detail at the end, as in a study that involves deception, or you may offer to send a summary of the results to those who wish to receive it. For example, "If you would like to receive a summary of the results of this research, please write your name and address in the space provided at the end of the questionnaire." (In this case the respondent would yield confidentiality, but his or her anonymity may be preserved.)

We have included in this chapter a sample letter of invitation (see Table 12.1) to participate in a dissertation study and a sample informed consent form (see Table 12.2). Note that some groups are simply not able to provide informed consent on their own. These include (but are not limited to) persons under 18 years of age, the mentally retarded, and the psychologically disabled. In these situations the informed consent form should be signed by the participant's parent or legal guardian.

BIAS-FREE WRITING

We conclude this chapter with a brief discussion of ethical issues in scholarly writing. Throughout the dissertation it is important to avoid language and materials that are oppressive or discriminatory to any group of people. Questionnaires and measures should be scrupulously checked to be certain that they do not imply that it is "normal" or "right" to belong to a specific ethnic group, have a particular sexual preference, or engage in a particular life-style.[1] Writers need to stay current with language that is sensitive to diverse groups because what was acceptable terminology yesterday may not

Table 12.1   Sample Letter of Invitation to Participate in a Research Project

---

CHILDHOOD TRAUMA AND PERSONALITY

I am currently involved in a research project addressing clinical issues related to childhood trauma and personality. The project examines the relationship of certain childhood experiences to specific heightened abilities. The study is performed as a partial fulfillment of the requirements for my Ph.D. degree in clinical psychology at the University of the North Pole.

Your participation in this project will provide useful information on this topic. You qualify for participation if you are between the ages of 18 and 65. You will be asked to complete five (5) brief true-false instruments that will take about 30 minutes. You will also be asked to fill out a background questionnaire and a childhood history survey that will take approximately 20 to 30 minutes.

Participation in this study is strictly voluntary. You may withdraw from the study at any point without penalty. Participation is not associated with your class grade. All data from this project are confidential and will be used for research purposes only. Data from questionnaires and instruments are anonymous. Names of participants will not be connected to information and scores.

Although there are no foreseeable risks to the participant, the childhood history survey contains detailed questions regarding family violence and abuse. If you feel questions of this type would upset you, please feel free to decline from participation at any point in this project.

Thank you for your assistance.

(Signature)
Name of researcher
Telephone number

---

be acceptable today. Here are a few guidelines to keep in mind in order to eliminate bias:

Substitute gender-neutral words and phrases for gender-biased words. A common mistake is the inadvertent use of sexist terms that are deeply entrenched in our culture, such as "chairman" instead of

Table 12.2   Informed Consent for Participation in Research Project

---

This study considers the relationship between childhood experiences and personality. It is performed as a partial fulfillment of the requirements for the researcher's Ph.D. in clinical psychology at the University of the North Pole.

There are no foreseeable risks with this research. If any discomfort should arise regarding material addressed in the study, participants can call a number (provided by the researcher) to ask questions or discuss these feelings. A more complete statement of the nature and purpose of the research will be available when the data collection is completed.

I agree to participate in this research project and I understand that:
1.   The time required for this study is about 60 minutes.
2.   The nature of my participation includes completing five (5) self-report measures, a background information sheet, and a childhood experience sheet.
3.   My participation is entirely voluntary. I may terminate my involvement at any time without penalty.
4.   All my data are confidential.
5.   All data are for research purposes only and will not affect my course grade.
6.   If I have questions about the research, or need to talk to the researcher after my participation in the study, I can contact the researcher by calling (telephone number) or writing to:

Name of researcher
Address of researcher

Signed _____ Date _____

"chairperson," "mothering" instead of "parenting," and "mankind" instead of "people" or "human beings."

Use designations in parallel fashion to refer to men and women equally. Example: "5 men and 14 women," *not* "5 men and 14 females."

Do not assume that certain professions are gender-related (e.g., "the scientist . . . he") and avoid sexual stereotyping (e.g., "a bright and beautiful female professor").

Avoid gender-biased pronouns (e.g., "A consultant may not always be able to see *his* clients"). A few nonsexist alternatives to this pervasive problem are:

- Add the other gender: *"his or her* clients." This alternative should be used only occasionally because it can become very cumbersome. It is, however, preferable to awkward constructions such as *s/he, him/her, her,* or *he(she).*
- Use the plural form: "Consultants . . . *their* clients"
- Delete the adjective: "to see clients"
- Rephrase the sentence to eliminate the pronoun: "Clients may not always be seen by their consultants."
- Replace the masculine or feminine pronouns with *one* or *you*

Do not identify people by race or ethnic group unless it is relevant. If it is relevant, try to ascertain the currently most acceptable terms and use them.

Avoid language that suggests evaluation or reinforces stereotypes. For example, referring to a group as "culturally deprived" is evaluative, and remarking that the "Afro-American students, *not surprisingly,* won the athletic events," reinforces a stereotype.

Don't make unsupported assumptions about various age groups (e.g., that the elderly are less intellectually able or are remarkable for continuing to work energetically).

NOTE

1. A thoughtful article by McHugh, Koeske, and Frieze (1986) describes how unintentional sexism may creep into the design of a study at the level of method, theory, or conceptualization and offers suggestions for excluding it.

References

American Psychological Association. (1983). *Publication manual of the American Psychological Association* (3rd. ed.). Washington, DC: Author.

American Psychological Association. (1990). Ethical principles of psychologists (amended June 2, 1989). *American Psychologist, 45,* 390-395.

Bailey, P. A. (1992). *A phenomenological study of the psychological transition from being a mother of dependent daughters to being a mother of adult daughters.* Unpublished doctoral dissertation, The Fielding Institute, Santa Barbara, CA.

Baron, R. M., & Kenny, D. A. (1986). The moderator-mediator variable distinction in social psychological research: Conceptual, strategic, and statistical considerations. *Journal of Personality and Social Psychology, 51,* 1173-1182.

Barrett, H. D. (1990). *Adult self-directed learning, personal computer competency and learning style: Models for more effective learning.* Unpublished doctoral dissertation, The Fielding Institute, Santa Barbara, CA.

Barth, P. A. (1987). *A study of the individuation process in women at the midlife transition.* Unpublished doctoral dissertation, The Fielding Institute, Santa Barbara, CA.

Becker, C. (1986). Interviewing in human science research. *Methods, 1,* 101-124.

Belenky, M., Clinchy, B., Goldberger, N., & Tarule, J. (1986). *Women's ways of knowing: The development of self, voice and mind.* New York: Basic Books.

Bell, M. (1988). *An introduction to the Bell Object Relations Reality Testing Inventory.* Unpublished manuscript, V. A. Medical Center, Psychology Service, West Haven, CT.

Bevan, W. (1991). Contemporary psychology: A tour inside the onion. *American Psychologist, 46,* 475-483.

Borgatta, E., & Bohrnstedt, G. (1981). Level of measurement: Once over again. In E. Borgatta & G. Bohrnstedt (Eds.), *Social measurement: Current issues.* Beverly Hills, CA: Sage.

Caddell, David P. (1989). *Moral education in the college environment.* Unpublished master's thesis, California State University, Fullerton.

Campbell, D. T., & Stanley, J. C. (1966). Experimental and quasi-experimental designs for research and teaching. In N. L. Gage (Ed.), *Handbook of research on teaching.* Chicago: Rand McNally.

Cohen, J. (1990). Things I have learned so far. *American Psychologist, 45,* 1304-1312.

Connell, D. (1992). *The relationship between Siddah meditation and stress in psychotherapists: A transpersonal perspective.* Doctoral dissertation, in progress, The Fielding Institute, Santa Barbara, CA.

Cook, T. D., & Campbell, D. T. (1979). *Quasi-experimentation: Design and analysis issues for field settings.* Chicago: Rand McNally.

Cronbach, L. J. (1975). Beyond the two disciplines of scientific psychology. *American Psychologist, 30,* 116-127.

Davenport, L. (1991). *Adaptation to dyslexia: Acceptance of the diagnosis in relation to coping efforts and educational plans.* Unpublished doctoral dissertation, The Fielding Institute, Santa Barbara, CA.

Douglas, Jack D. (1985). *Creative interviewing.* Beverly Hills, CA: Sage.

Dumas, C. (1989). *Daughters in family-owned business: An applied systems perspective.* Unpublished doctoral dissertation, The Fielding Institute, Santa Barbara, CA.

Ewing, N. R. (1992). *Psychodevelopmental influences in augmentation mammoplasty.* Unpublished doctoral dissertation, The Fielding Institute, Santa Barbara, CA.

Feyerabend, P. K. (1981a). *Philosophical papers. Vol. 1: Realism, rationalism, and scientific method.* Cambridge, UK: Cambridge University Press.

Feyerabend, P. K. (1981b). *Philosophical papers. Vol. 2: Problems of empiricism.* Cambridge, UK: Cambridge University Press.

Gefland, H., & Walker, C. J. (1990). *Mastering APA style: Student's workbook and training guide.* Washington, DC: American Psychological Association.

Gergen, M. (1988). Toward a feminist metatheory and methodology in the social sciences. In M. M. Gergen (Ed.), *Feminist thought and the structure of knowledge.* New York: New York University Press.

Gigerenzer, G. (1991). From tools to theory: A heuristic of discovery in cognitive psychology. *Psychological Review, 98,* 254-267.

Giorgi, A. (1985). *Phenomenology and psychological research.* Pittsburgh, PA: Harper & Row.

Glaser, B. G., & Strauss, A. L. (1967). *The discovery of grounded theory: Strategies for qualitative research.* Chicago: Aldine/Atherton.

Goffman, E. (1961). *Asylums.* Garden City, NY: Anchor.

Goldberg, N. (1991). *Writing down the bones/Wild mind.* New York: Quality Paperback Book Club.

Guba, E. (1981). Criteria for assessing the trustworthiness of naturalistic inquiries. *Educational Communication and Technology Journal, 29,* 75-92.

Guba, E., & Lincoln, Y. S. (1981). *Effective evaluation.* San Francisco: Jossey-Bass.

Hamilton, L. (1990). *Modern data analysis: A first course in applied statistics.* Pacific Grove, CA: Brooks/Cole.

Hardwick, C. (1990). *Object relations and reality testing in adult children of alcoholics: An exploratory and descriptive study.* Unpublished doctoral dissertation, The Fielding Institute, Santa Barbara, CA.

Harlow, D. D., & Linet, M. S. (1989). Agreement between questionnaire data and medical records. *American Journal of Epidemiology, 129,* 233-248.

Hewson, D., & Bennett, A. (1987). Childbirth research data: Medical records or women's reports? *American Journal of Epidemiology, 125,* 484-491.

Holmes, T., & Rahe, R. (1967). The Social Readjustment Rating Scale. *Journal of Psychosomatic Research, 11,* 213-218.

Honan, P., & Devlin, J. (1990, August). Word Processing. *Personal Computing, 14*(8).

Horwitz, R. I. (1986). Comparison of epidemiological data from multiple sources. *Journal of Chronic Disease, 39*, 889-896.

Hoshmand, L. T. (1989). Alternate research paradigms: A review and teaching proposal. *Counseling Psychologist, 17*, 3-79.

Human and Organization Development Knowledge Area Study Guides. (1991). Santa Barbara, CA: The Fielding Institute.

Kachigan, S. K. (1986). *Statistical analysis: An introduction to univariate and multivariate statistics for the social sciences.* New York: Radius Press.

Kazdin, A. E. (1992). *Research design in clinical psychology* (2nd ed.). New York: Harper & Row.

Keen, E. (1975). *A primer in phenomenological psychology.* Lanham, MD: University Press of America.

Kerlinger, F. N. (1977). *Foundations of behavioral research* (3rd ed.). New York: Holt, Rinehart & Winston.

Kerlinger, F. N. (1979). *Behavioral research: A conceptual approach.* New York: Holt, Rinehart & Winston.

Kranzberg, M. (1988). *Heterosexual and lesbian relationships of elective lesbians.* Unpublished doctoral dissertation, The Fielding Institute, Santa Barbara, CA.

Kratochwill, T. R. (Ed.). (1978). *Strategies to evaluate changes in the single subject.* New York: Academic Press.

Knowledge Index. Palo Alto, CA: Dialog Information Systems, Inc.

Kuhn, T. (1962). *The structure of scientific revolutions.* Chicago: University of Chicago Press.

Lauriston, R. (1990). Hard disk health insurance. *PC World, 8*(7).

Lazarus, R. S., & Folkman, S. (1984). *Stress, appraisal and coping.* New York: Springer.

Leon, J. M. (1991). *Family and peer relations of delinquent juvenile gang members and non-gang members.* Unpublished doctoral dissertation, United States International University, San Diego, CA.

Lincoln, Y. S., & Guba, E. G. (1985). *Naturalistic inquiry.* Beverly Hills, CA: Sage.

Locke, L. F., Spirduso, W. W., & Silverman, S. J. (1987). *Proposals that work: A guide for planning dissertations and grant proposals.* Newbury Park, CA: Sage.

Macdonald, S. (1990). *Empathy, personal maturity, and emotional articulation.* Unpublished doctoral dissertation, The Fielding Institute, Santa Barbara, CA.

Mahoney, M. J. (1990). *Human change processes.* New York: Basic Books.

Mann, T. (1987). *A guide to library research methods.* New York: Oxford University Press.

Marshall, C., & Rossman, G. B. (1989). *Designing qualitative research.* Newbury Park, CA: Sage.

McHugh, M. C., Koeske, R. D., & Frieze, I. H. (1986). Issues to consider in conducting non-sexist psychological research. *American Psychologist, 41*, 879-890.

McNamara, D. (1991). *Toward a model of optimal family development: A paradigm based in psychosynthesis and developed from general systems theory.* Unpublished doctoral dissertation, The Fielding Institute, Santa Barbara, CA.

Miles, M. B., & Huberman, A. M. (1984). *Qualitative data analysis: A sourcebook of new methods.* Beverly Hills, CA: Sage.

Mishler, E. G. (1986). *Research interviewing: Context and narrative.* Cambridge, MA: Harvard University Press.

Monserrat, C. (1989). *The adoption/relinquishment process in adolescent pregnancy.* Unpublished doctoral dissertation, The Fielding Institute, Santa Barbara, CA.

Moos, R. H. (1985, August 27). *Work as a human context.* Master Lecture, American Psychological Association Annual Convention, Los Angeles, CA.

National Opinion Research Center. (1988). *General social survey.* Chicago: Author.

National Opinion Research Center. (1990). *General social survey.* Chicago: Author.

Neighbors, J. (1991). *Factors influencing psychologists' attitudes towards education and training.* Unpublished doctoral dissertation, United States International University, San Diego, CA.

New, N. (1989). *Professional identity and gender: Impact on private practice management procedures.* Unpublished doctoral dissertation, United States International University, San Diego, CA.

Newton, S. G. (1991). *The incidence of depression, substance abuse, and eating disorders in the families of anorexic probands.* Unpublished doctoral dissertation, The Fielding Institute, Santa Barbara, CA.

Paape, J. (1992). *Health values and expectancies as predictors of preventive health behavior, health risk-taking behavior and risk-mix.* Unpublished doctoral dissertation, The Fielding Institute, Santa Barbara, CA.

Packer, M. J. (1985). Hermeneutic inquiry in the study of human conduct. *American Psychologist, 40,* 1081-1093.

Paganini-Hill, A., & Ross, P. K. (1982). Reliability of recall of drug usage and other health-related information. *American Journal of Epidemiology, 116,* 114-122.

Papyrus: The new standard in personal bibliographic databases. Salt Lake City, UT: Reference Systems.

Patterson, G. R., DeBaryshe, B. D., & Ramsey, E. (1989). A developmental perspective on antisocial behavior. *American Psychologist, 44,* 329-335.

Patton, M. Q. (1980). *Qualitative evaluation methods.* Beverly Hills, CA: Sage.

Peplau, L. A., & Conrad, E. (1989). Beyond nonsexist research: The perils of feminist methods in psychology. *Psychology of Women Quarterly, 13,* 379-400.

Polkinghorne, D. E. (1983). *Methodology for the human sciences: Systems of inquiry.* Albany: SUNY Press.

Polkinghorne, D. E. (1989). Phenomenological research methods. In R. S. Valle & S. Halling (Eds.), *Existential-phenomenological perspectives in psychology.* New York: Plenum.

Polkinghorne, D. E. (1991). Two conflicting calls for methodological reform. *Counseling Psychologist, 19,* 103-114.

Popper, K. (1965). *Conjectures and refutations: The growth of scientific knowledge.* New York: Harper & Row.

Quittner, A. L., Glueckauf, R. L., & Jackson, D. N. (1990). Chronic parenting stress: Moderating versus mediating effects of social support. *Journal of Personality and Social Psychology, 59*(6), 1266-1278.

Rasche, C. (1991). *The yearning for a child in midlife women.* Unpublished doctoral dissertation, The Fielding Institute, Santa Barbara, CA.

Rennie, D. L., Phillips, J. R., & Quartaro, G. K. (1988). Grounded theory: A promising approach to conceptualization in psychology. *Canadian Psychology, 29,* 139-150.

Richards, N. (1991). *School-based assessment of students at risk for drug abuse.* Unpublished doctoral dissertation, United States International University, San Diego, CA.

Rico, G. L. (1983). *Writing the natural way.* Los Angeles: J. P. Tarcher.

Rogers, S. J., Parcel, T. L., & Menaghan, E. G. (1991). The effects of maternal working conditions and mastery on child behavior problems: Studying the intergenerational transmission of social control. *Journal of Health and Social Behavior, 32*(2), 145-164.

Sangster, M. J. (1991). *Judgment and decision making under conditions of uncertainty.* Unpublished doctoral dissertation, The Fielding Institute, Santa Barbara, CA.

Schutz, W. C. (1966). *FIRO: A three dimensional theory of interpersonal behavior.* Palo Alto, CA: Science and Behavior Books.

Searight, H. R. (1990). The neglect of qualitative evaluation in psychological training: Issues and alternatives. *Journal of Training and Practice in Professional Psychology, 4*(2), 33-43.

Seiden, R. H. (1966). Campus tragedy: A study of student suicide. *Journal of Abnormal and Social Psychology, 71* (389-399).

Selye, H. (1956). *The stress of life.* New York: McGraw-Hill.

Shallenberger, D. (1986). *Coming out at work.* Unpublished doctoral dissertation, The Fielding Institute, Santa Barbara, CA.

Shapiro, J. J., & Nicholsen, S. (1986). *Guidelines for writing papers.* Santa Barbara, CA: The Fielding Institute.

Slanger, E. (1991). *A model of physical risk-taking.* Unpublished doctoral dissertation, The Fielding Institute, Santa Barbara, CA.

Smith, M. B. (1991). *Human science—Really!* Invited symposium address, American Psychological Association Annual Convention, San Francisco, CA.

Spradley, J. P. (1979). *The ethnographic interview.* New York: Holt, Rinehart & Winston.

Sutherland, E. (1924). *Principles of criminology.* Philadelphia: W. B. Saunders.

Tabachnik, B. G., & Fidell, L. S. (1989). *Using multivariate statistics* (2 ed.). New York: Harper & Row.

Toulmin, S. (1972). *Human understanding: The collective use and evolution of concepts.* Princeton, NJ: Princeton University Press.

Volkman, N. (1991). *Belonging, A study of home and homelessness: A contribution to a theory of personality.* Unpublished doctoral dissertation. The Fielding Institute, Santa Barbara, CA.

Wardell, W. (1985). *The reunion of the male prison inmate with his family.* Unpublished doctoral dissertation, The Fielding Institute, Santa Barbara, CA.

Wegmann, M. F. (1992). *Information processing deficits of the authoritarian mind.* Unpublished doctoral dissertation, The Fielding Institute, Santa Barbara, CA.

Williams, R. L. (1989). *Finding voice: The transition from individualism to social advocacy.* Unpublished doctoral dissertation, The Fielding Institute, Santa Barbara, CA.

Winograd, T., & Flores, F. (1986). *Understanding computers and cognition: A new foundation for design.* Norwood, NJ: Ablex.

Name Index

Subject Index

About the Authors

Rae R. Newton, Professor of Sociology at California State University Fullerton, received his doctoral degree in Sociology from the University of California, Santa Barbara, and postdoctoral training at Indiana University. His research interests focus on measurement issues in the social sciences and children's mental health. His publications include articles in *The Journal of Personality Assessment, Educational and Psychological Measurement,* and *Sex Roles.*

Kjell Erik Rudestam is Program Director at The Fielding Institute, Santa Barbara, California. He was previously Professor of Psychology at York University, Toronto. Dr. Rudestam received his Ph.D. in Psychology from the University of Oregon. He is the author of *Methods of Self-Change, Experiential Groups in Theory and Practice,* and *Treating the Multi-Problem Family* (with Mark Frankel), as well as numerous articles in professional journals. His research interests are in the areas of suicide, psychotherapy, and family and organizational systems. He is a licensed clinical psychologist and a Diplomate of the American Board of Examiners in Professional Psychology (Clinical).

Jody Veroff is a faculty member in the Psychology and the Human and Organizational Development Programs at The Fielding Institute in Santa Barbara, California. She completed her doctoral degree in Clinical Psychology at the University of Michigan. She has had a lifelong interest in writing and currently devotes a large proportion of her work to writing critiques of students' essays and doctoral dissertations. Current interests include gender issues in research, multicultural education, and the exploration of the interface between family and organizational systems. Her publications include a book coauthored with Joseph Veroff, *Social Incentives: A Life-Span Developmental Approach.*

NOTES

NOTES

NOTES

NOTES

NOTES

NOTES

NOTES